this rawnasan TRASH art sketchbook

for bad drawings only!

belongs to

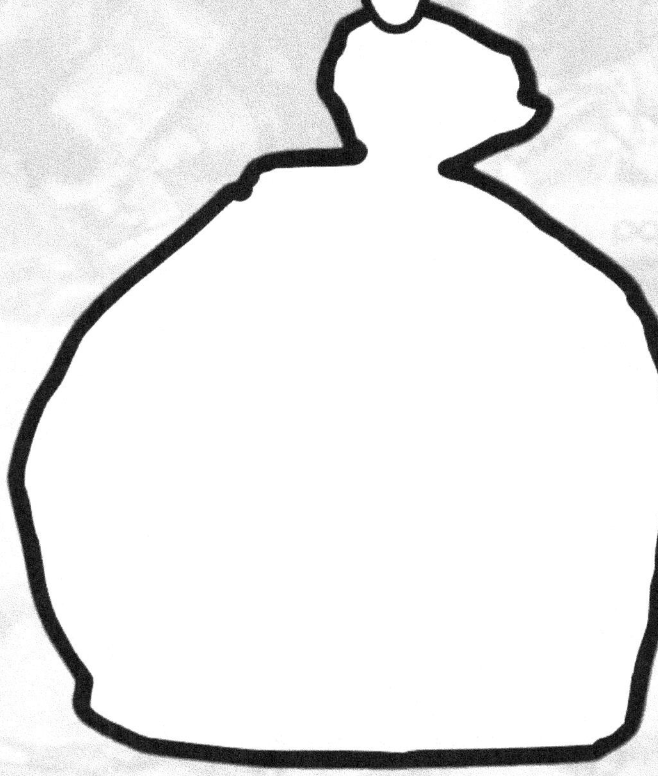

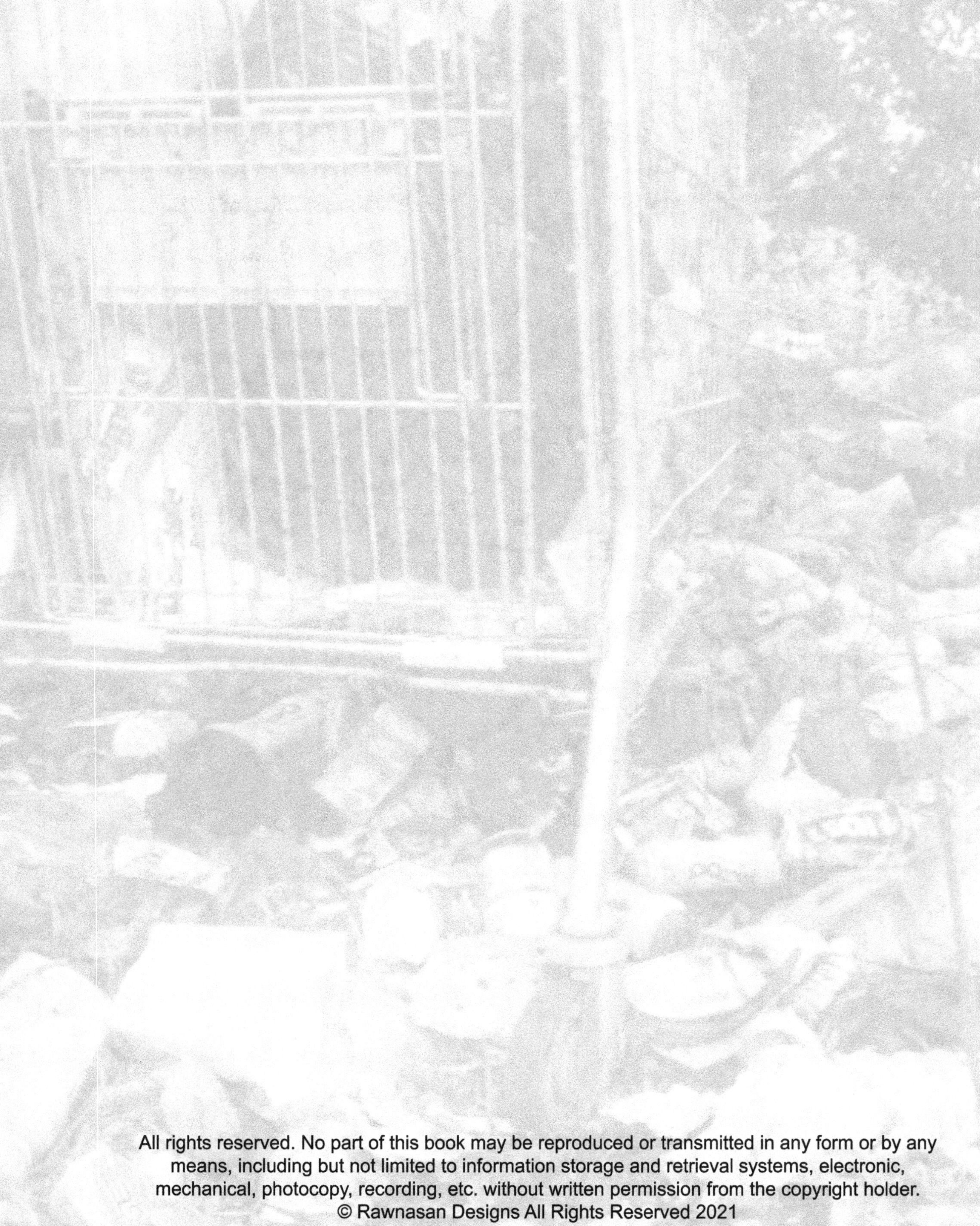

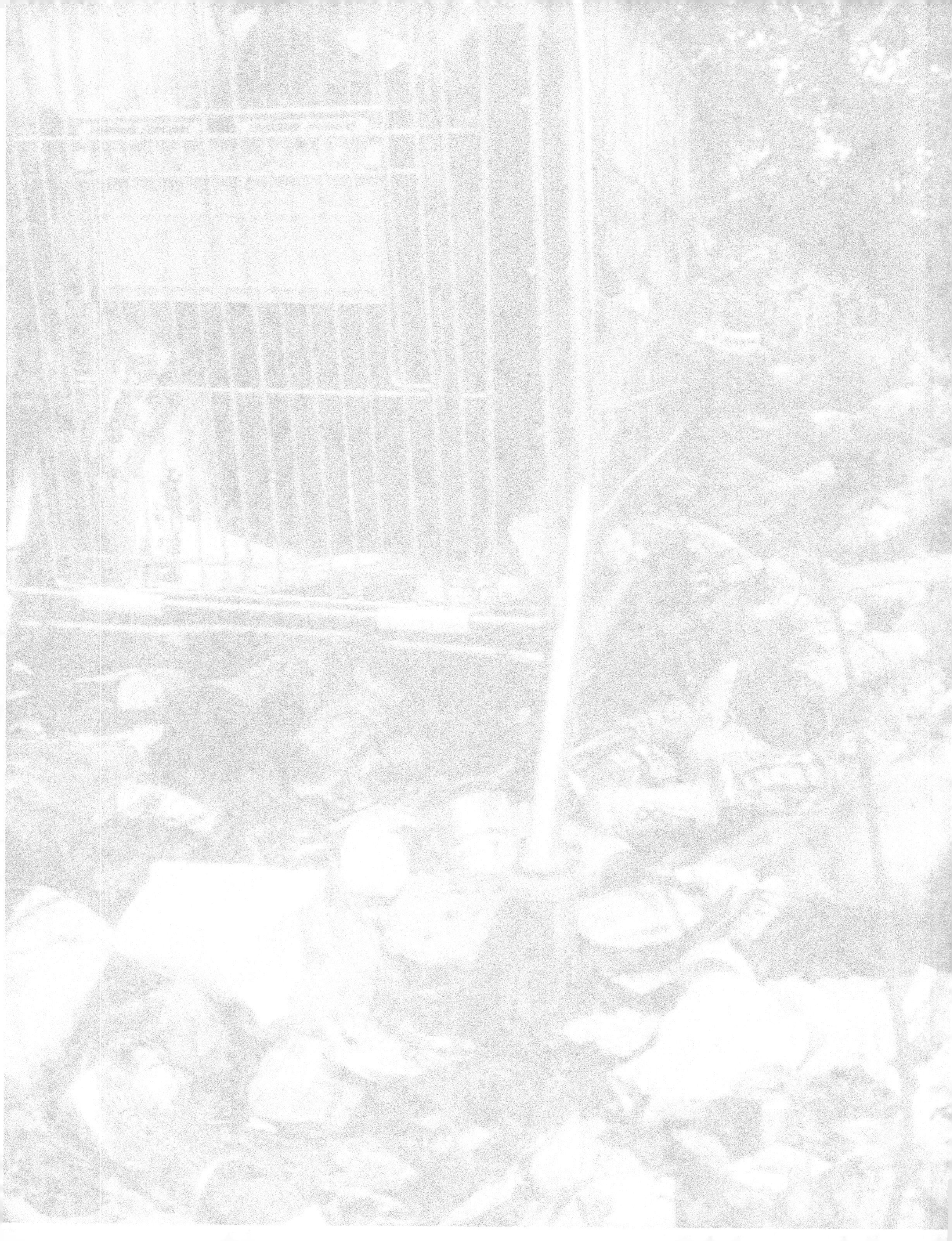

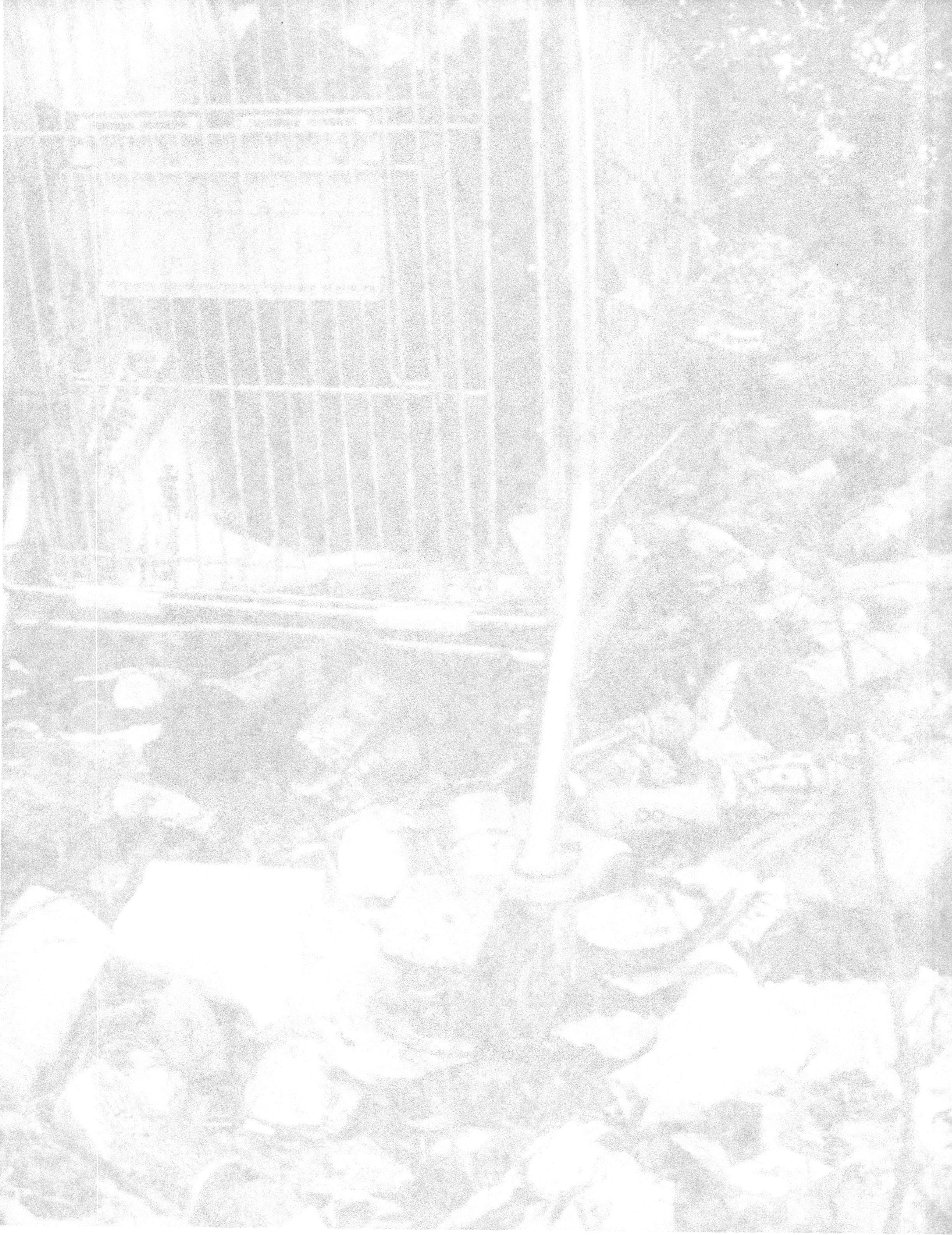

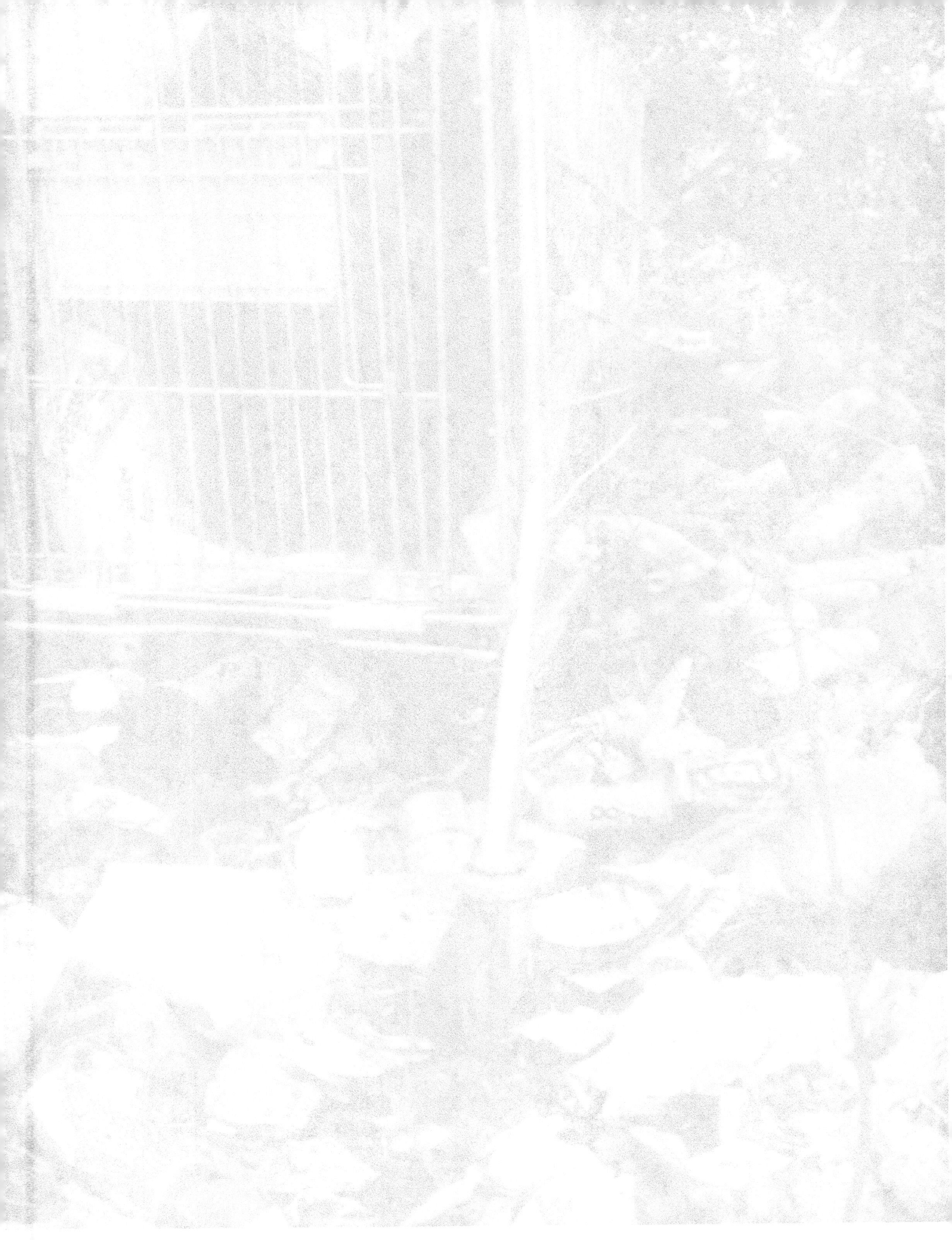

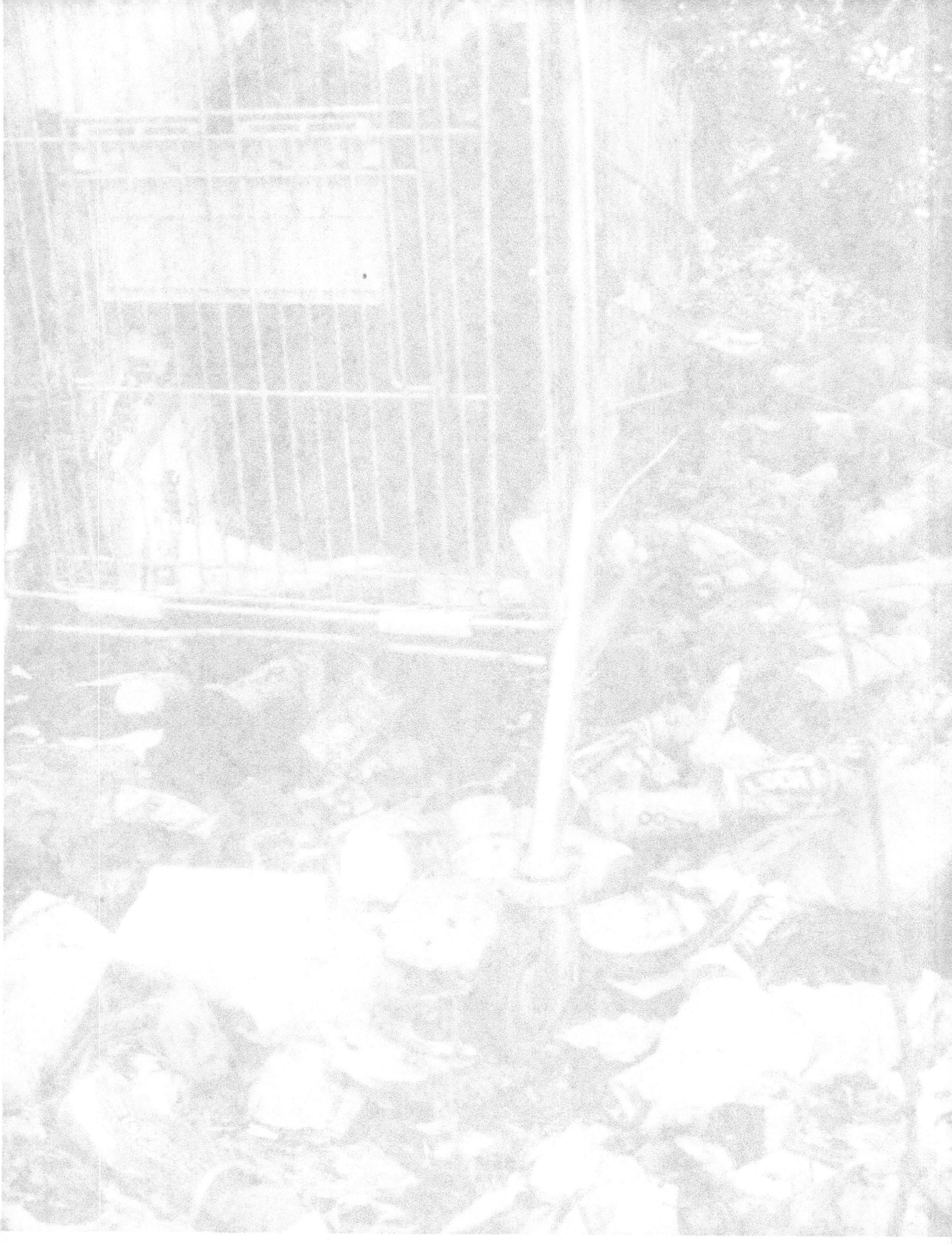

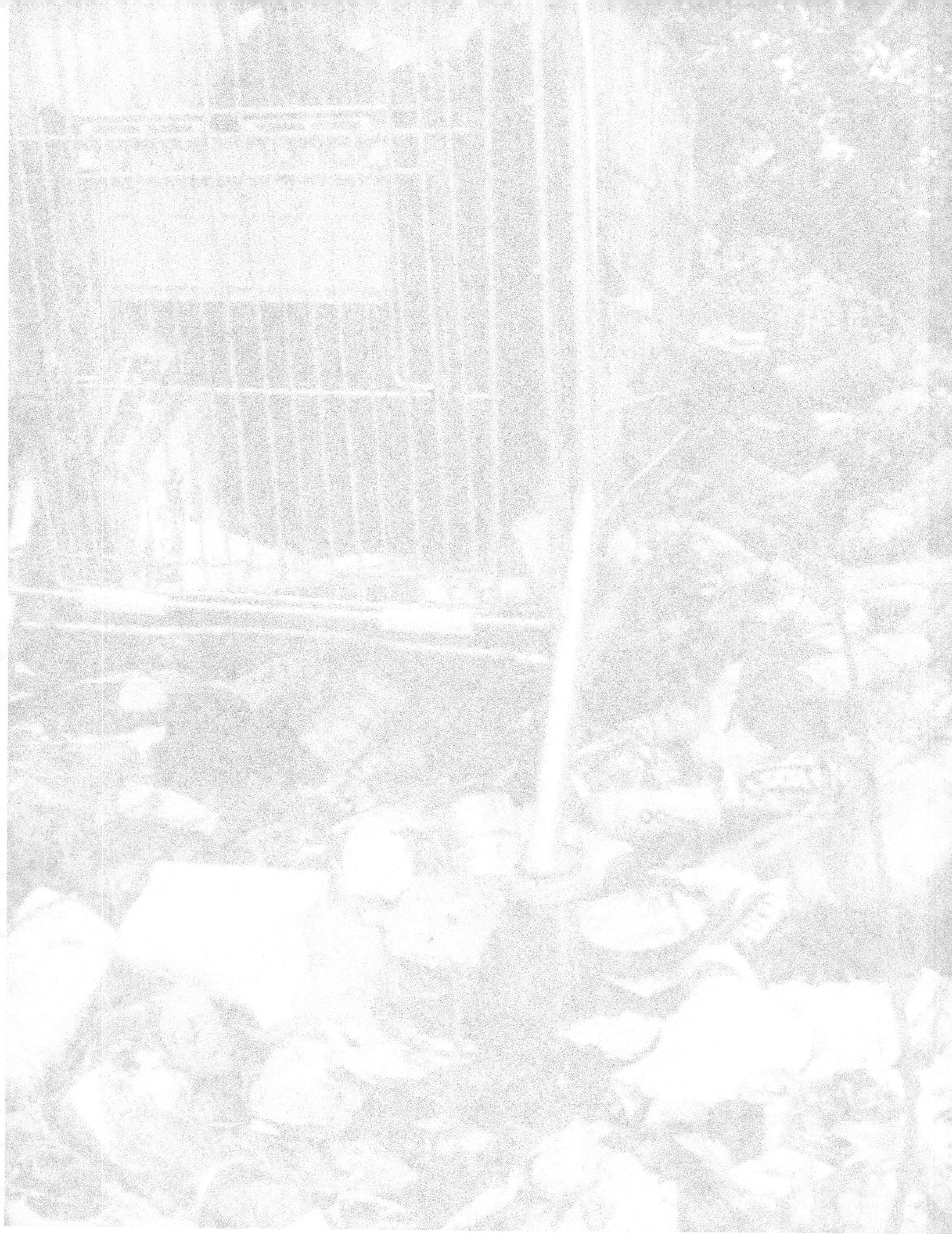

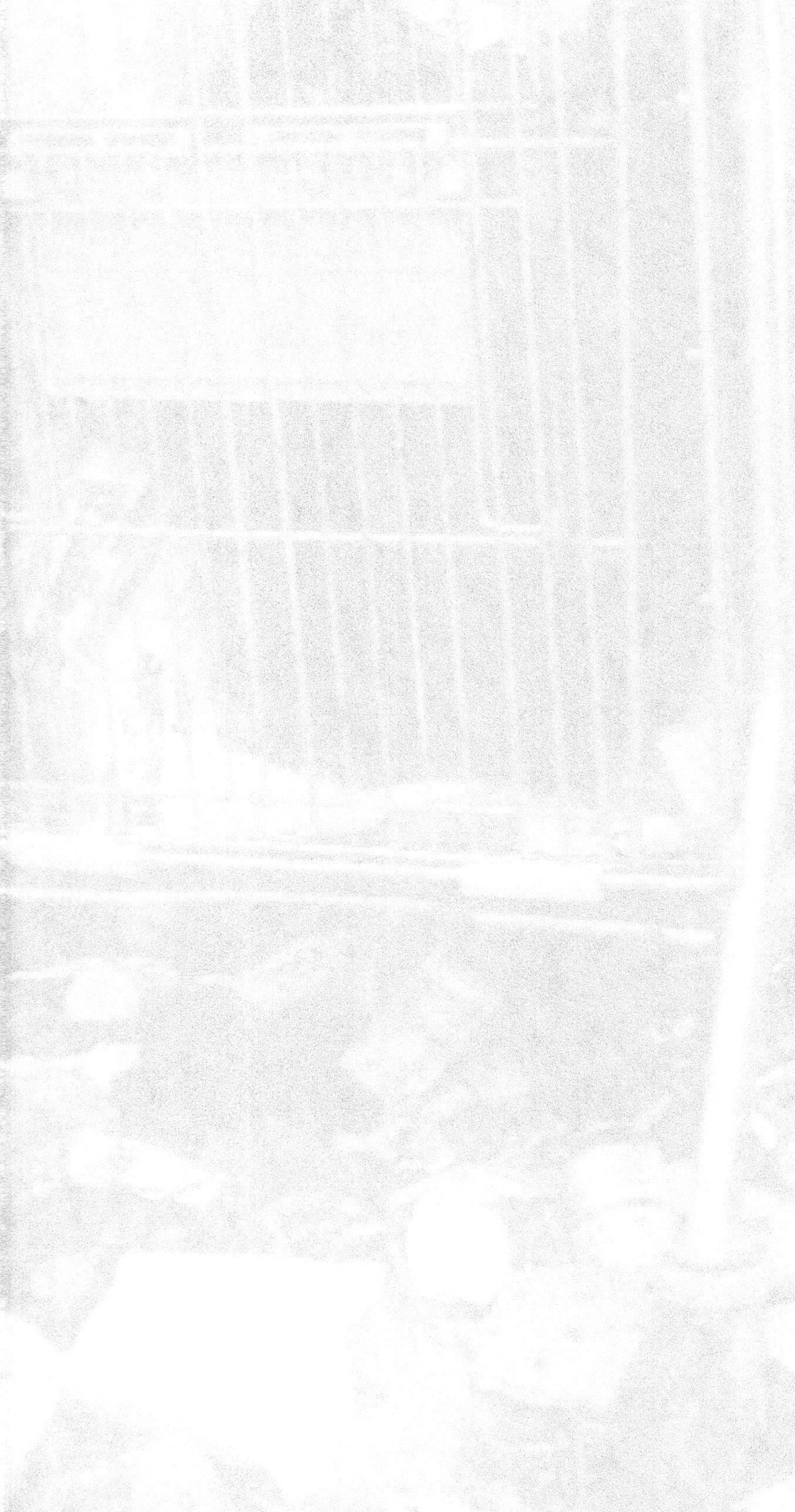

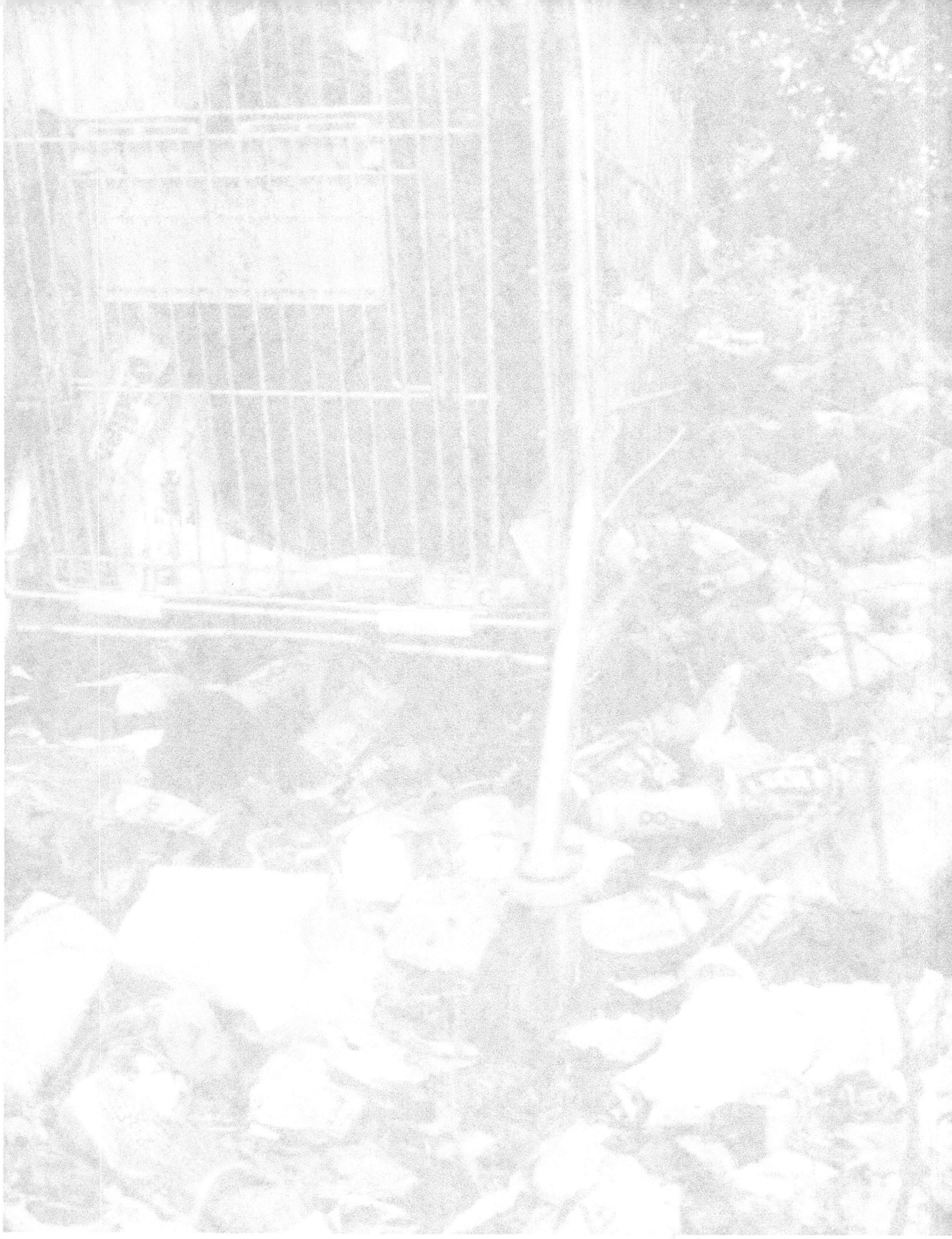

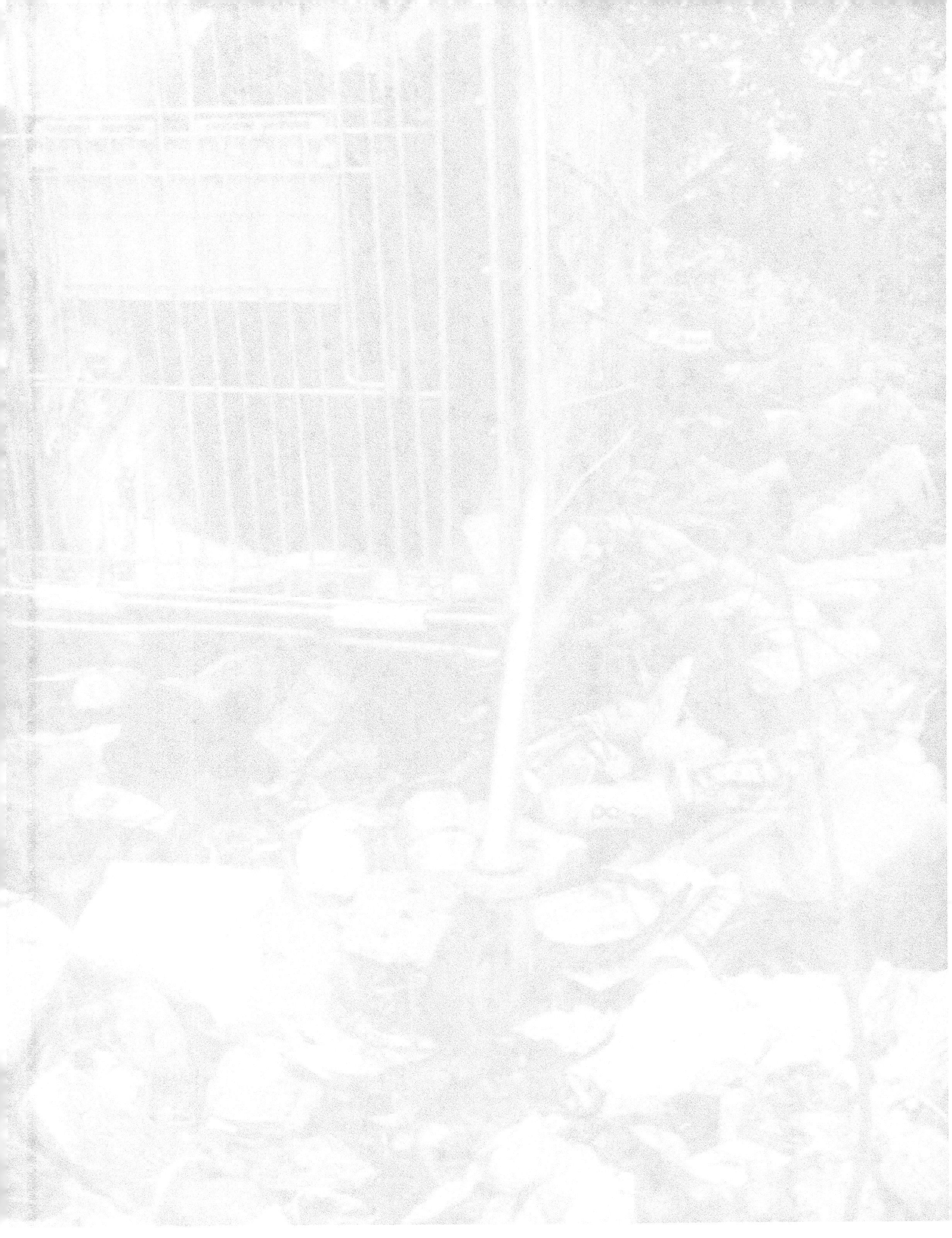

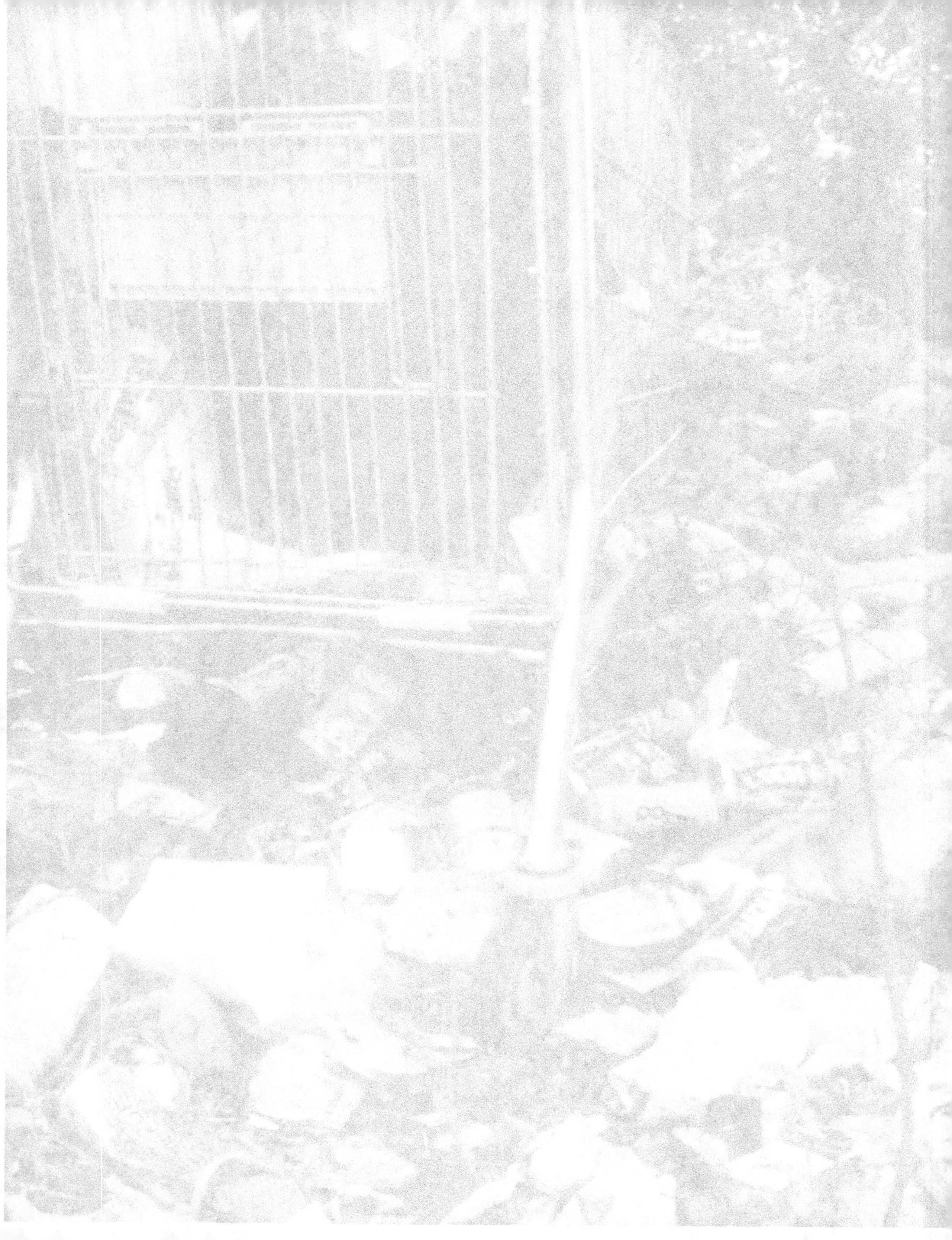

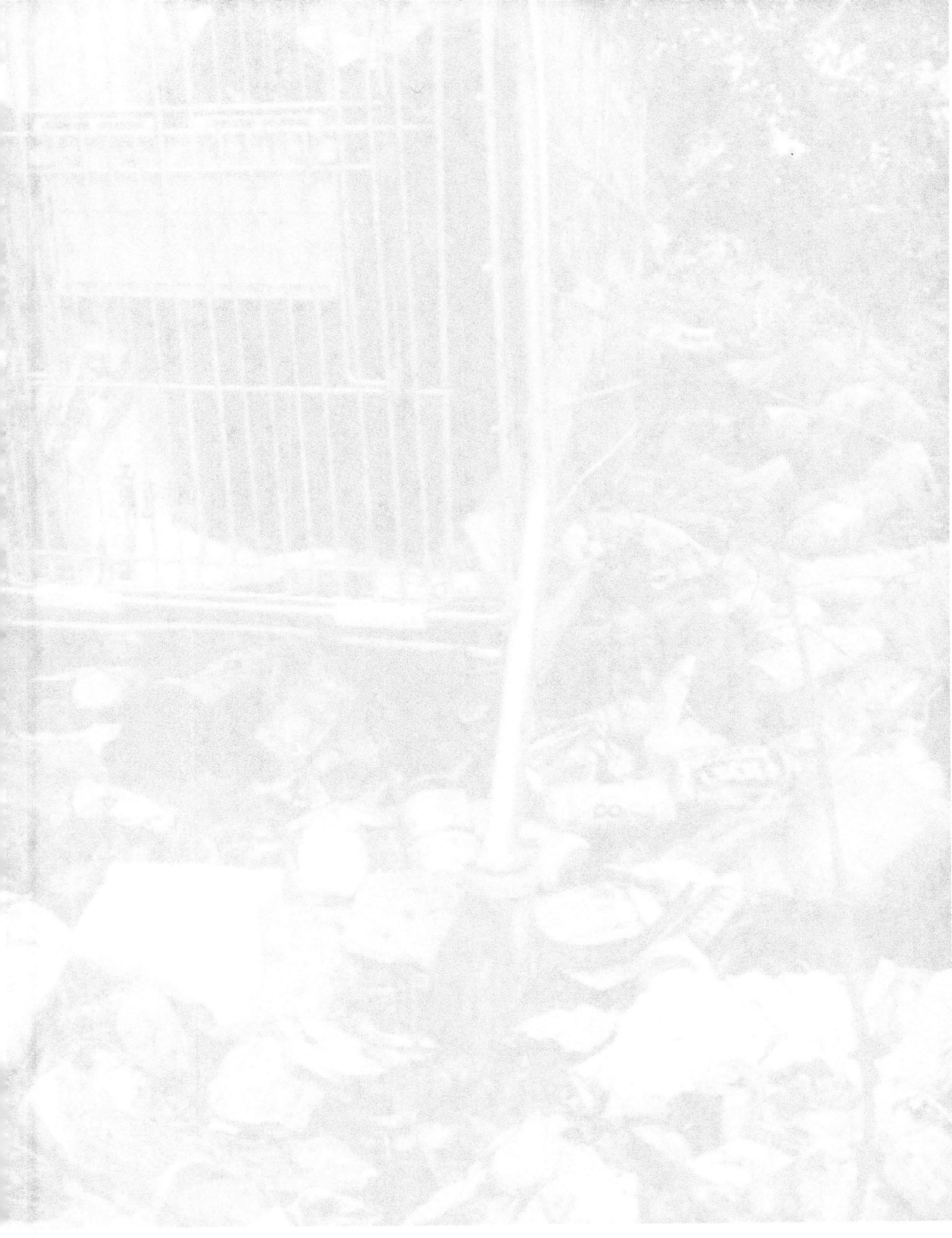

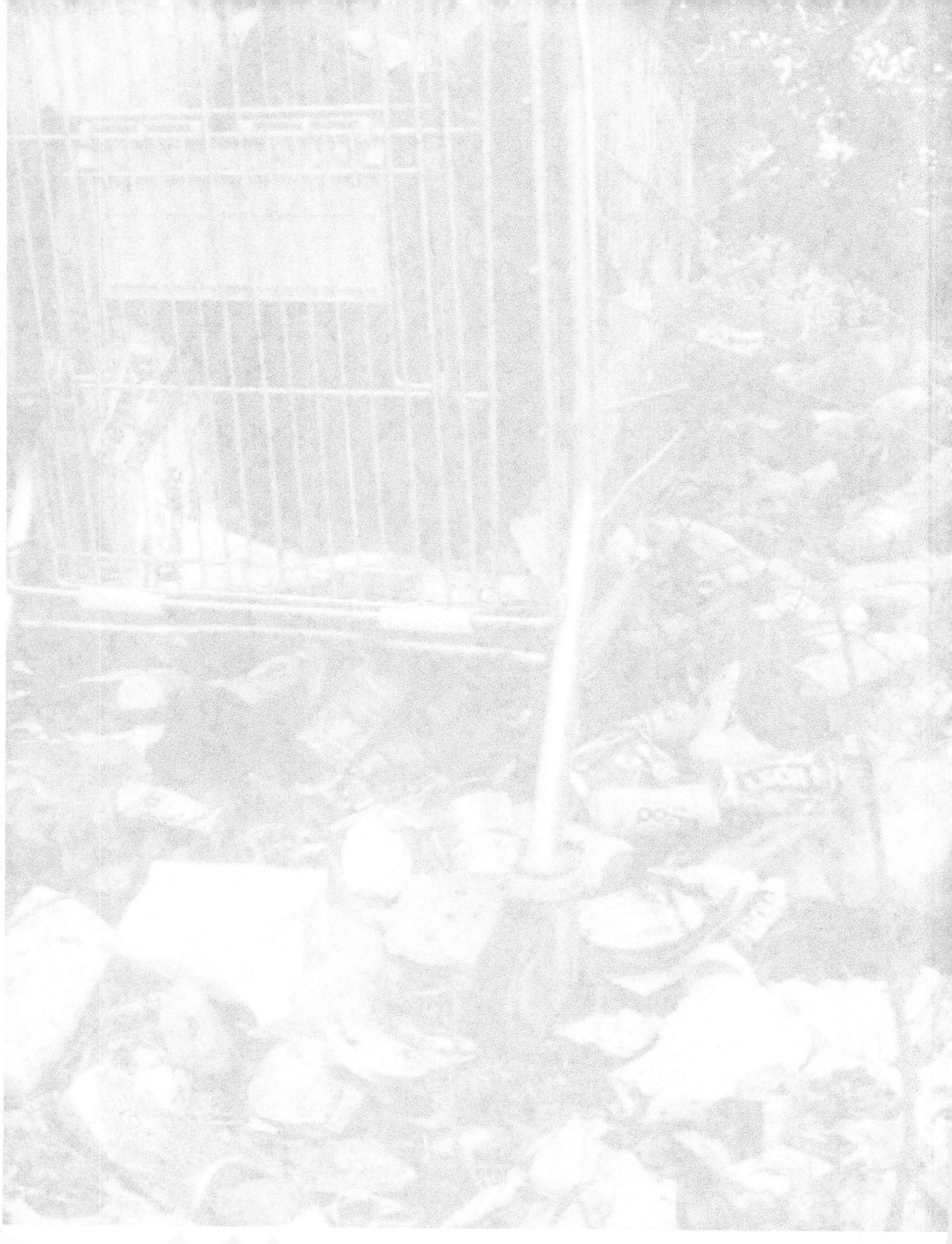

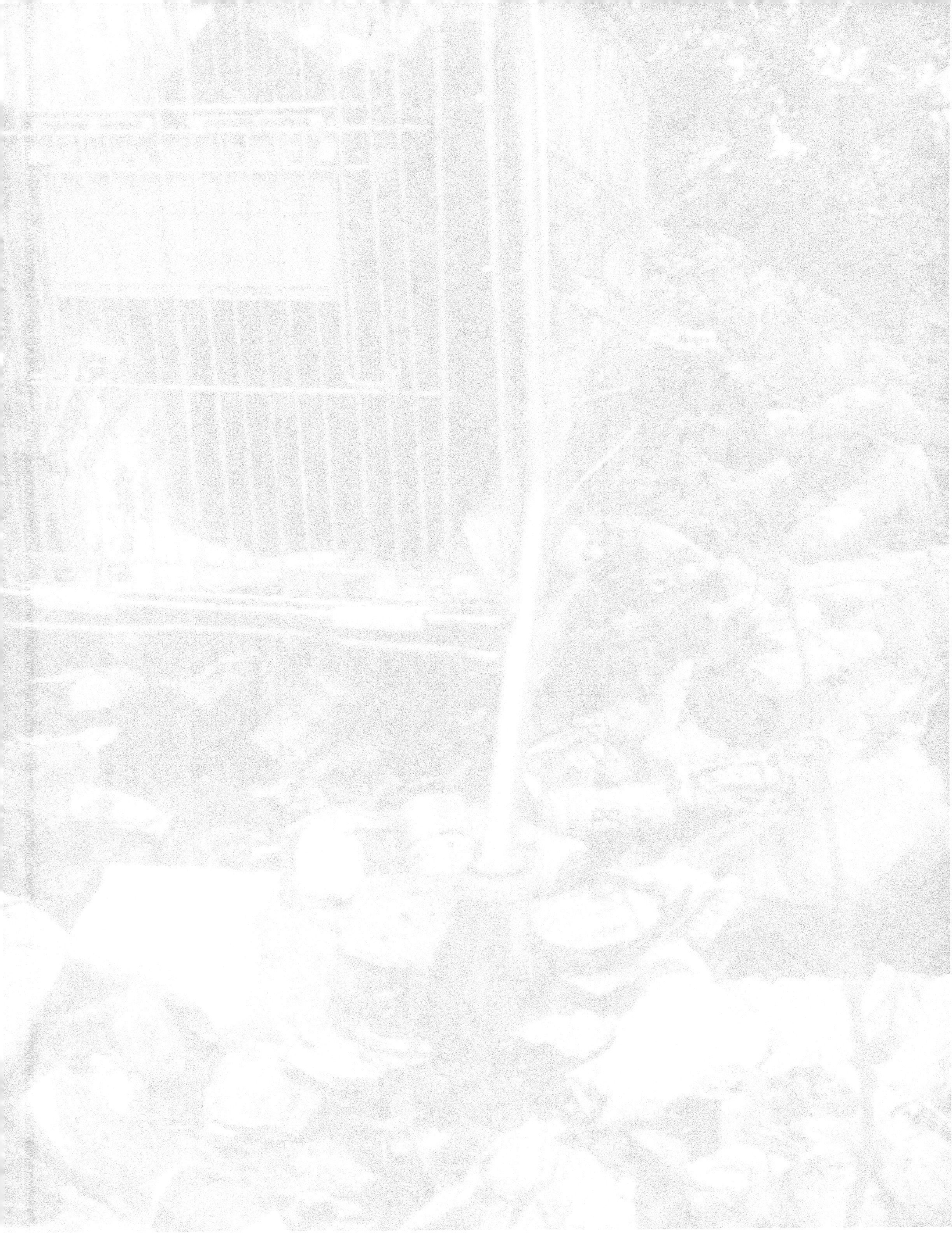

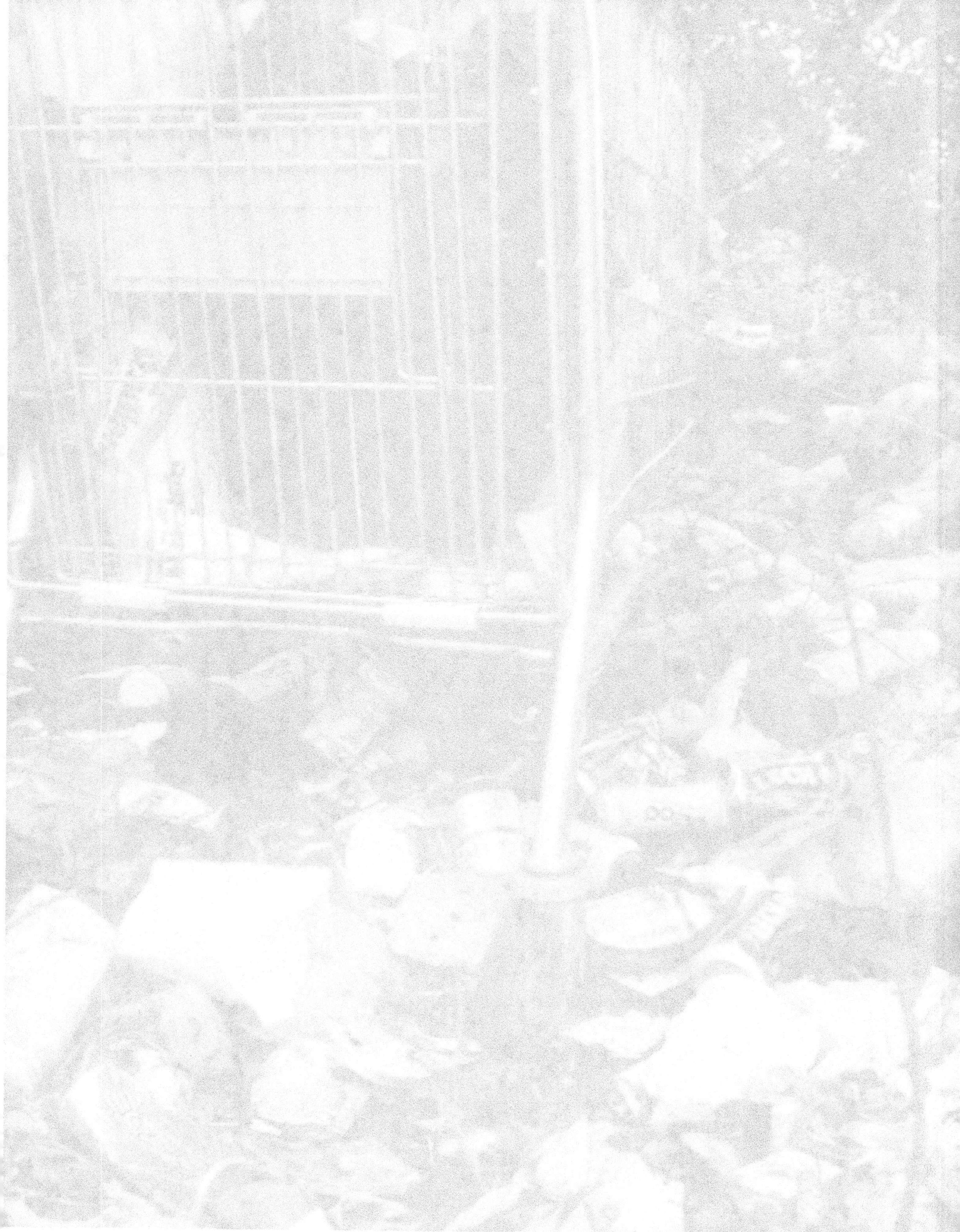

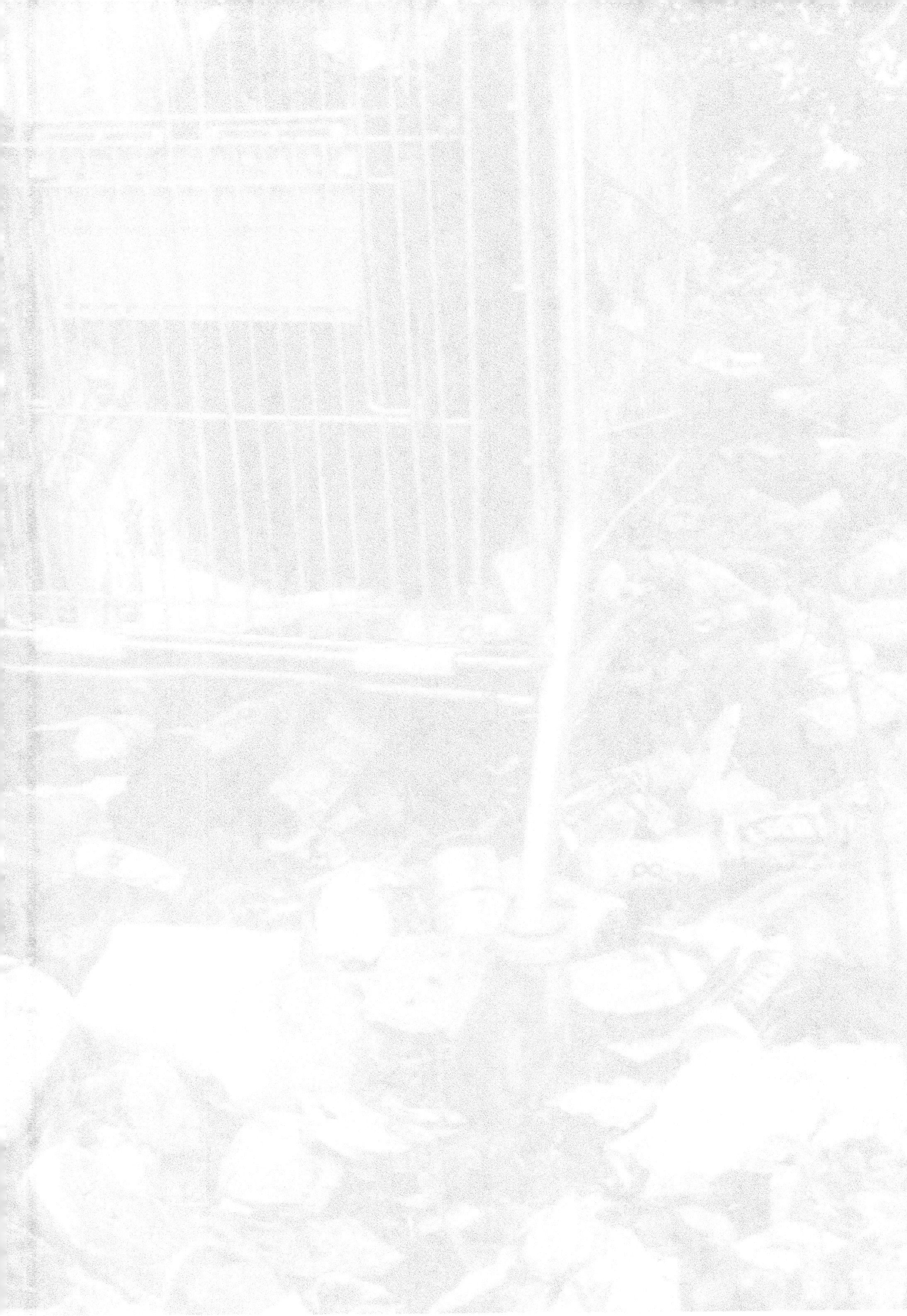

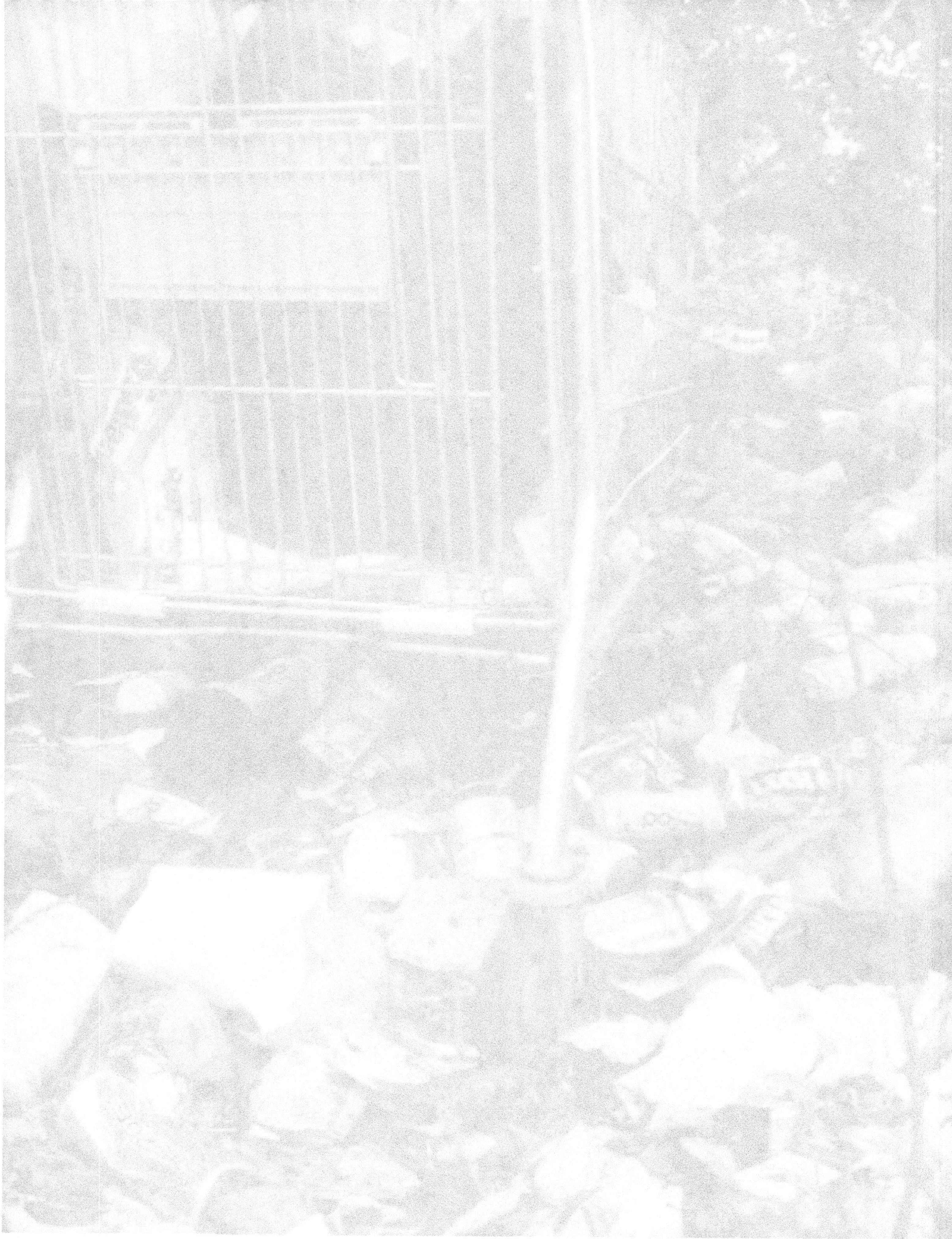

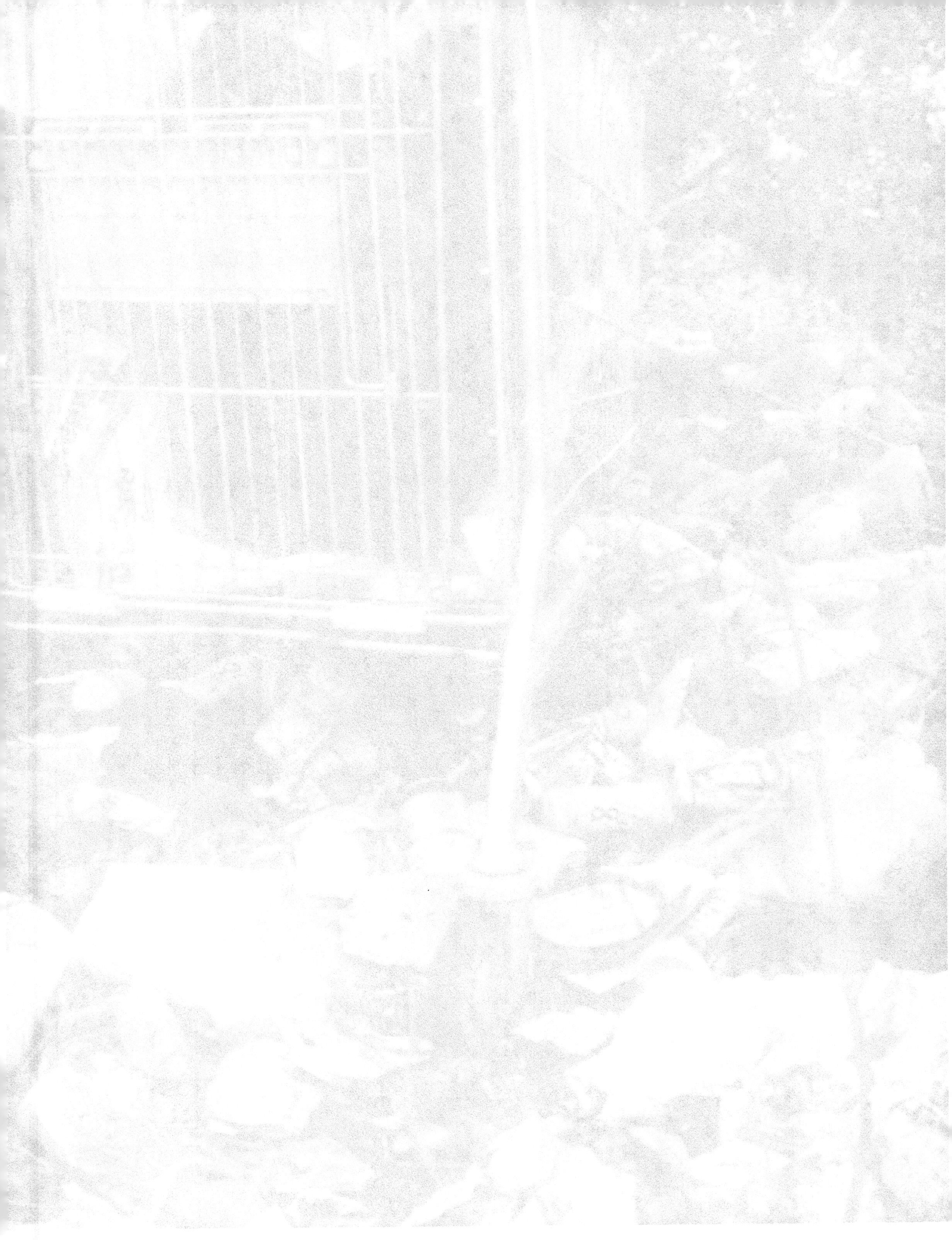

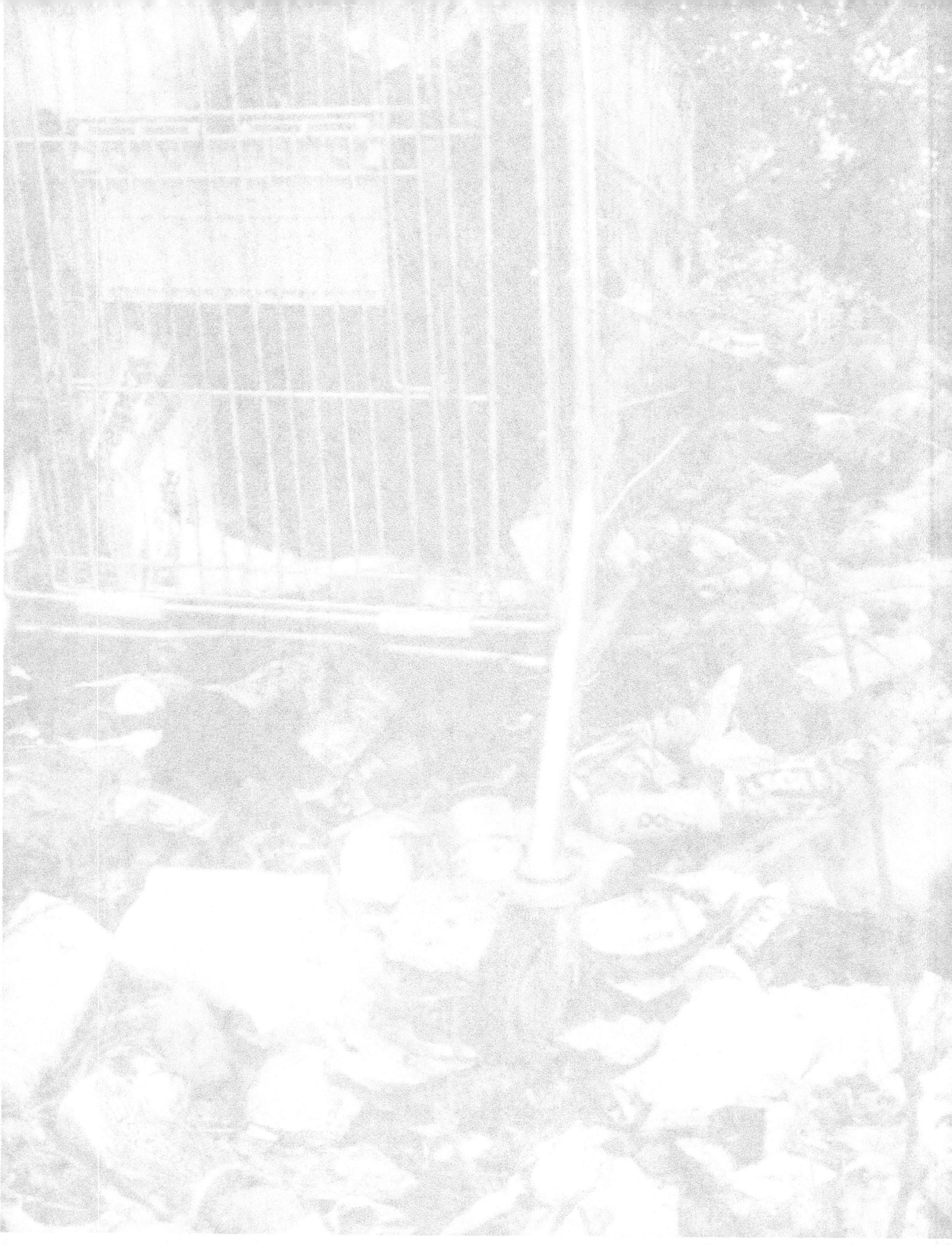

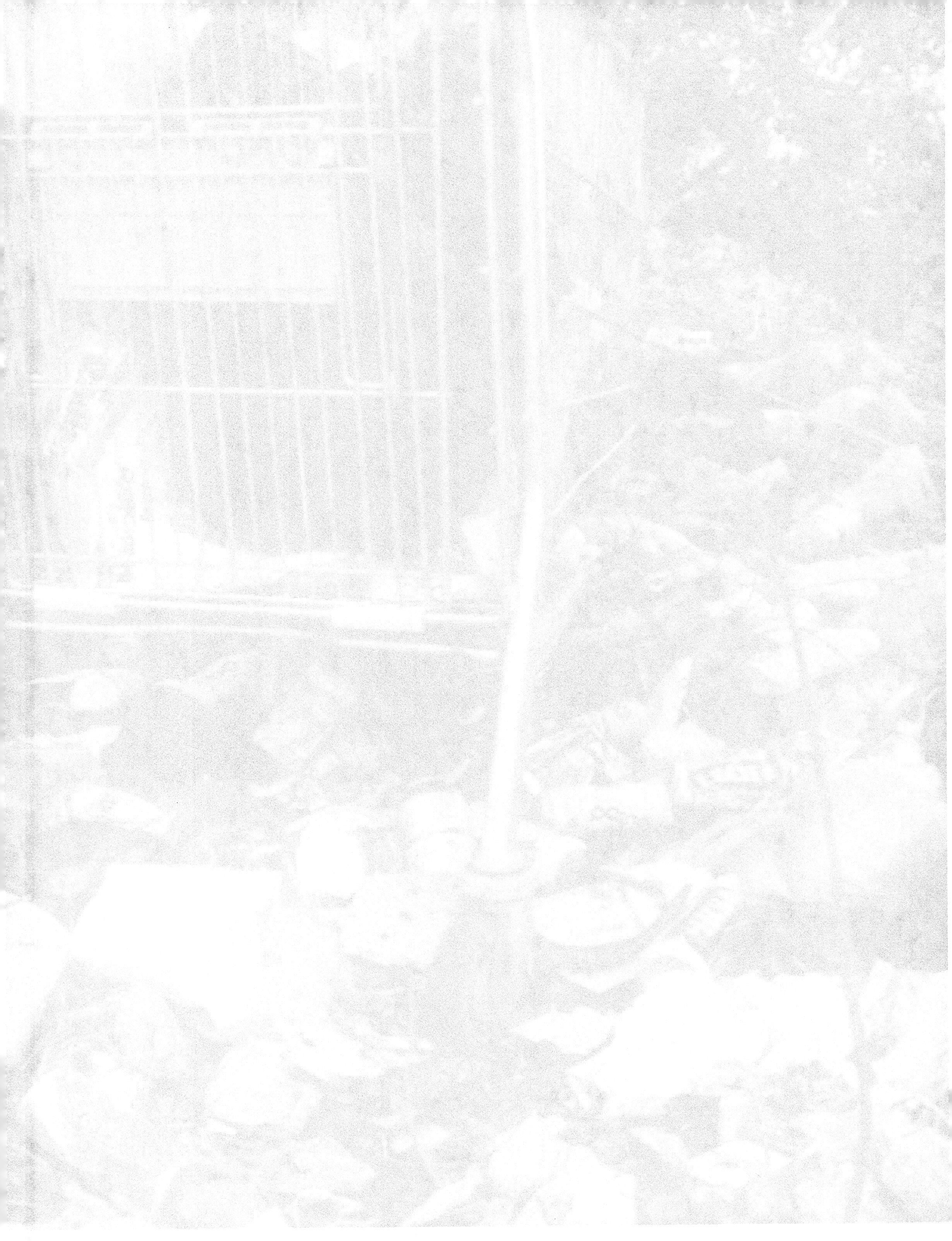

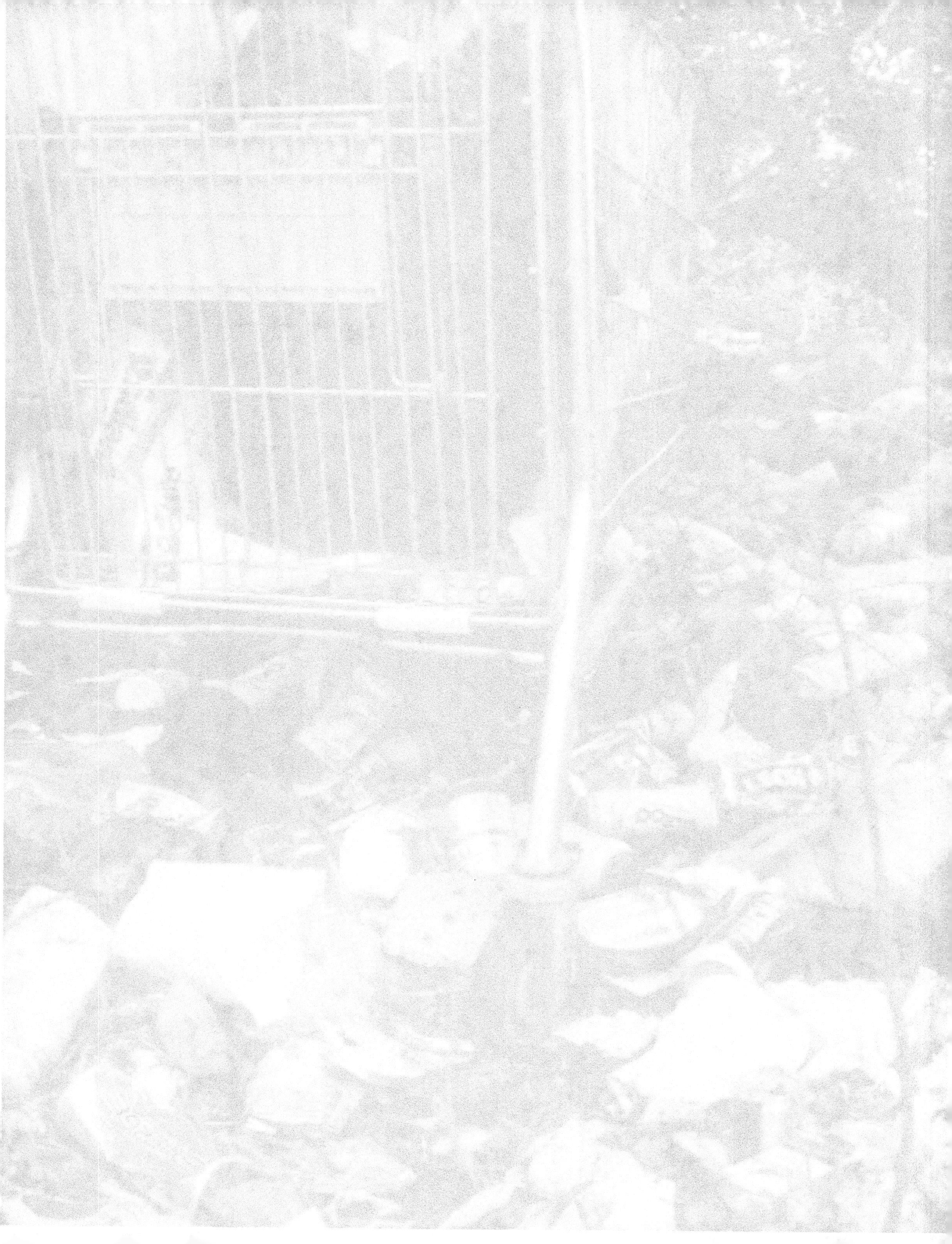

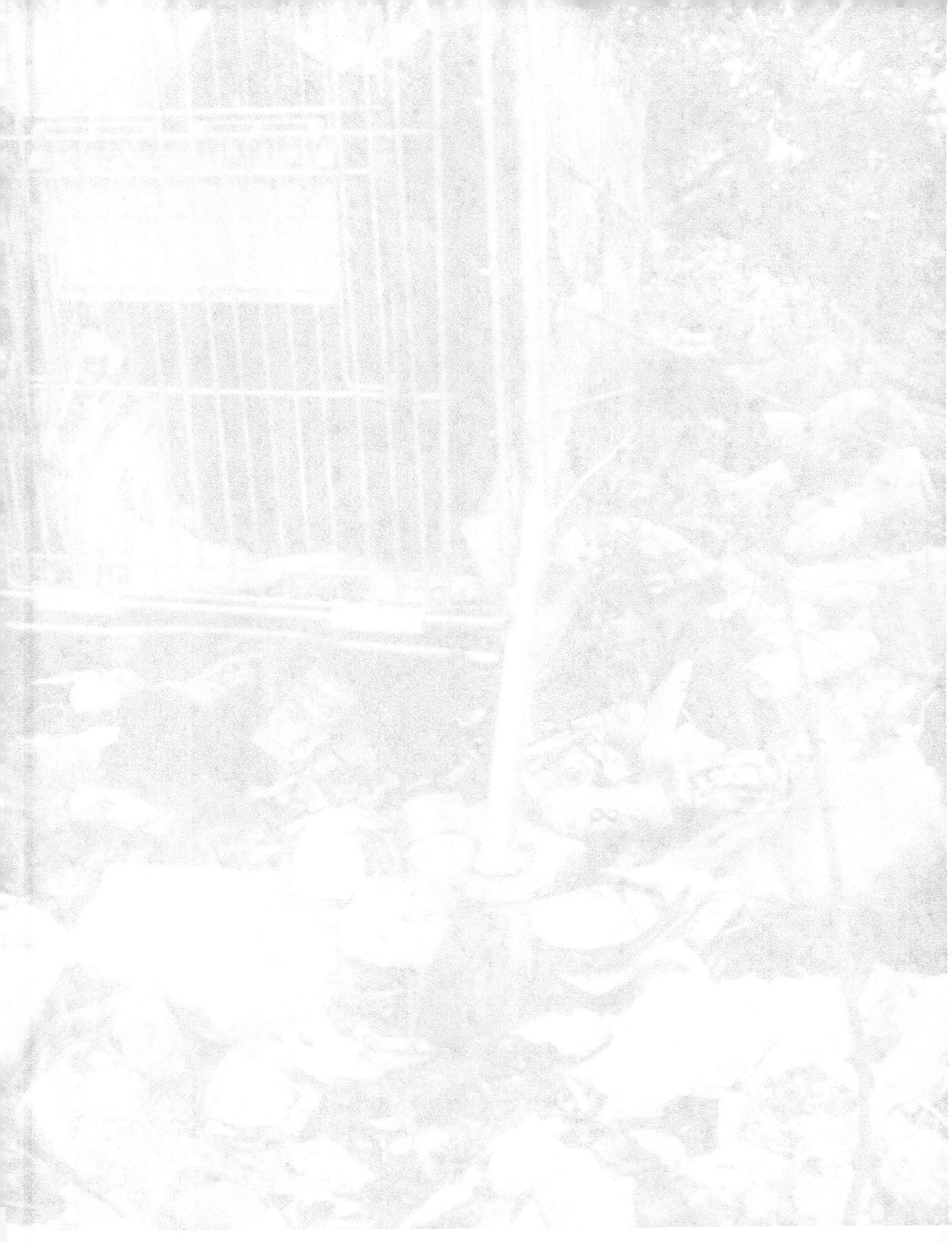

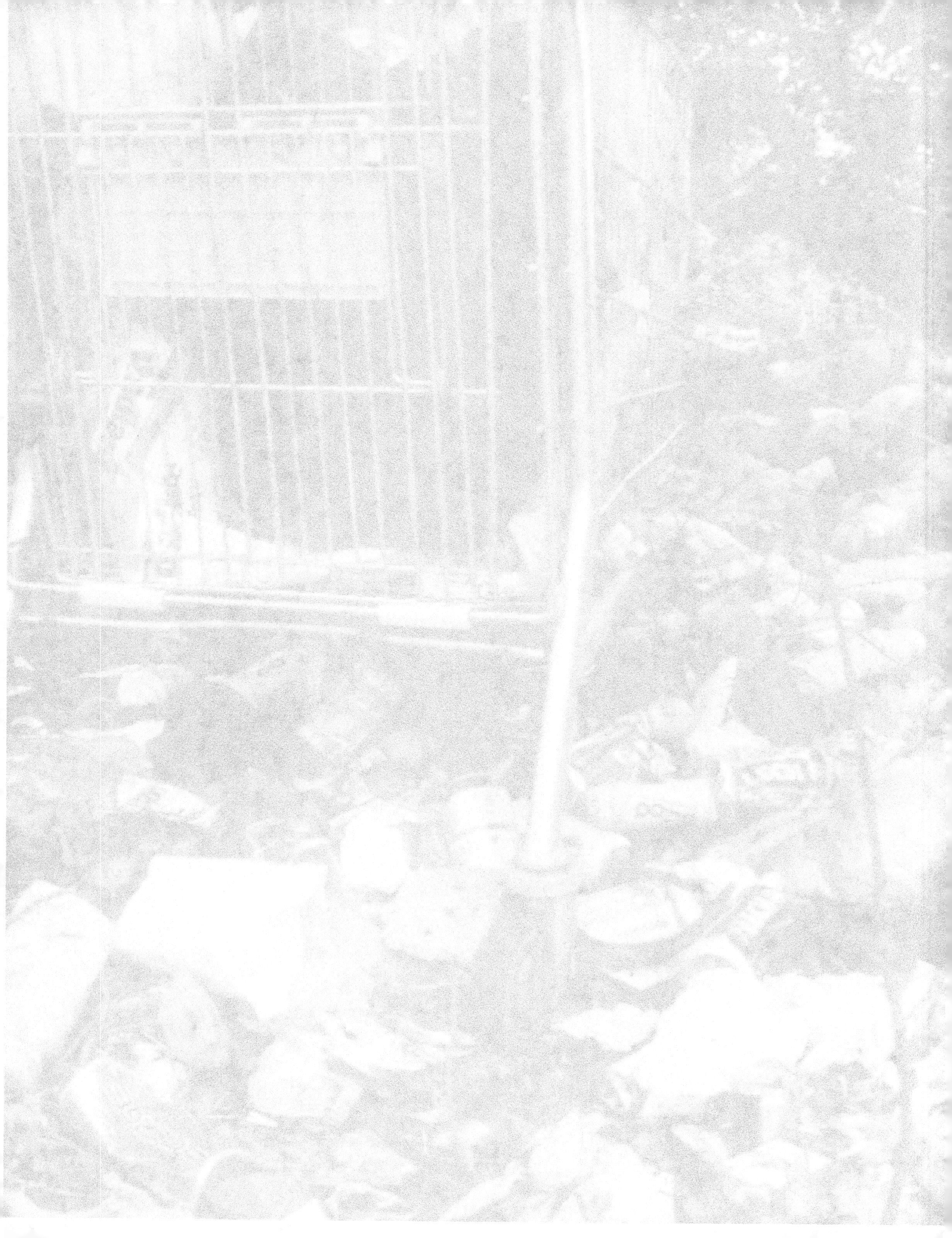

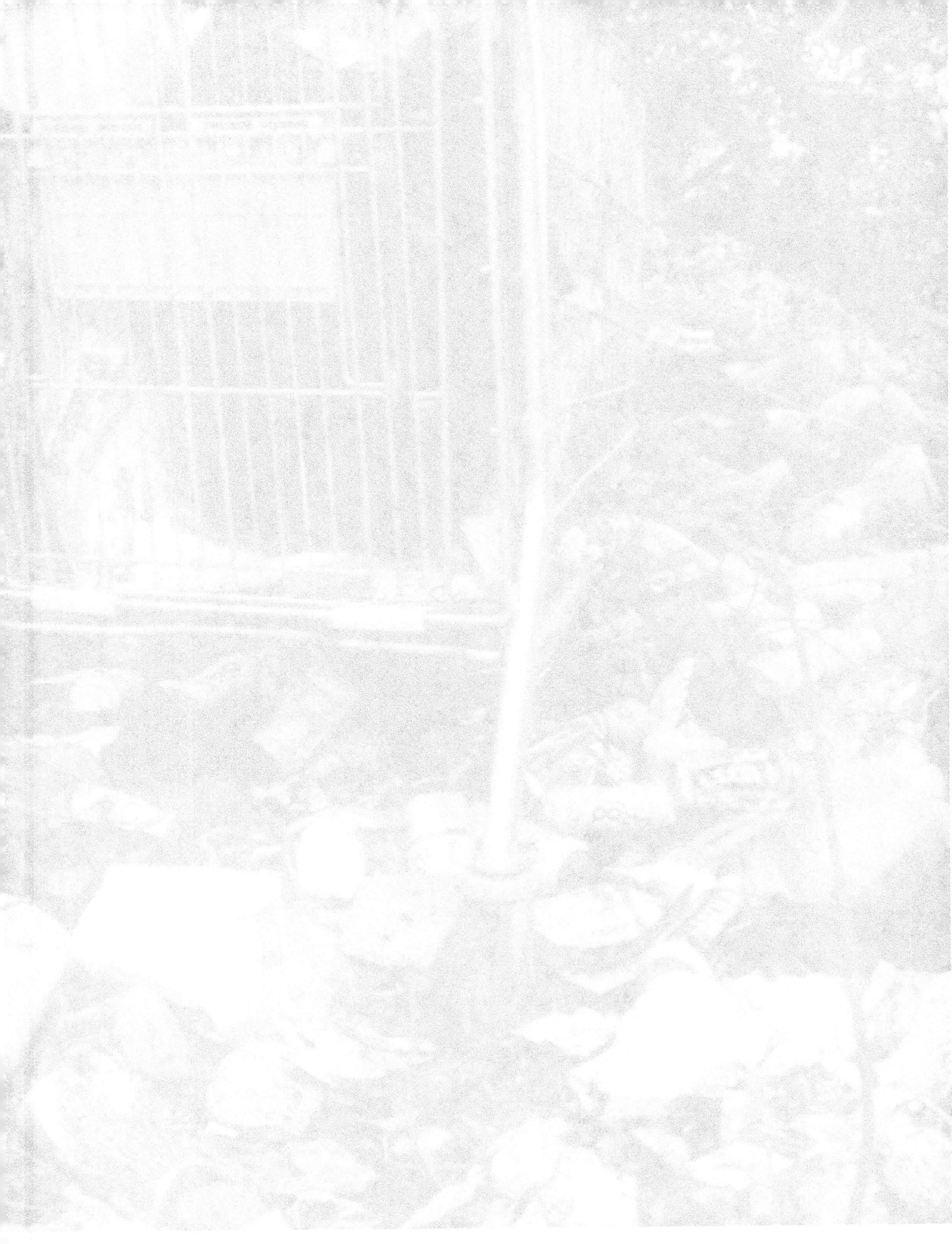

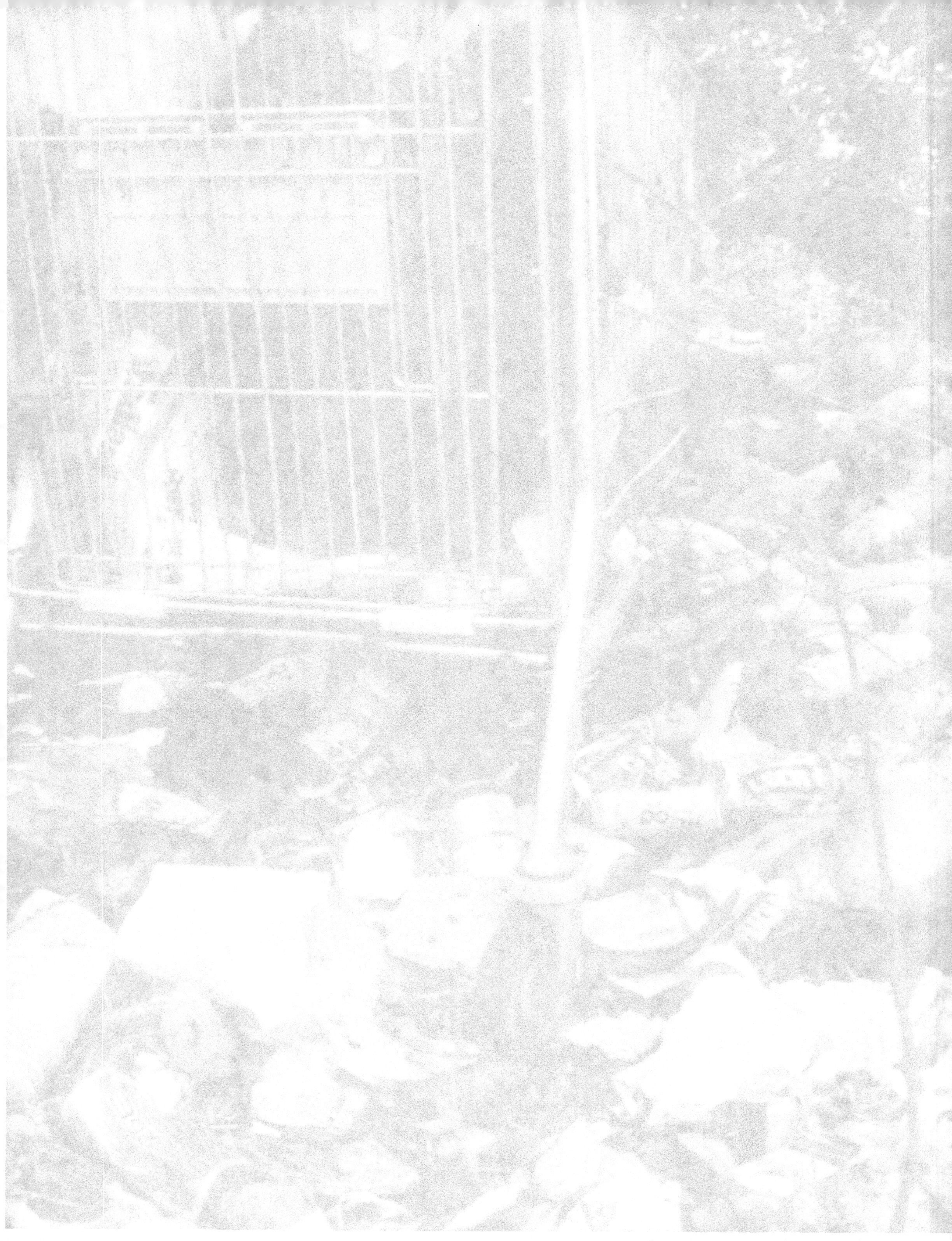

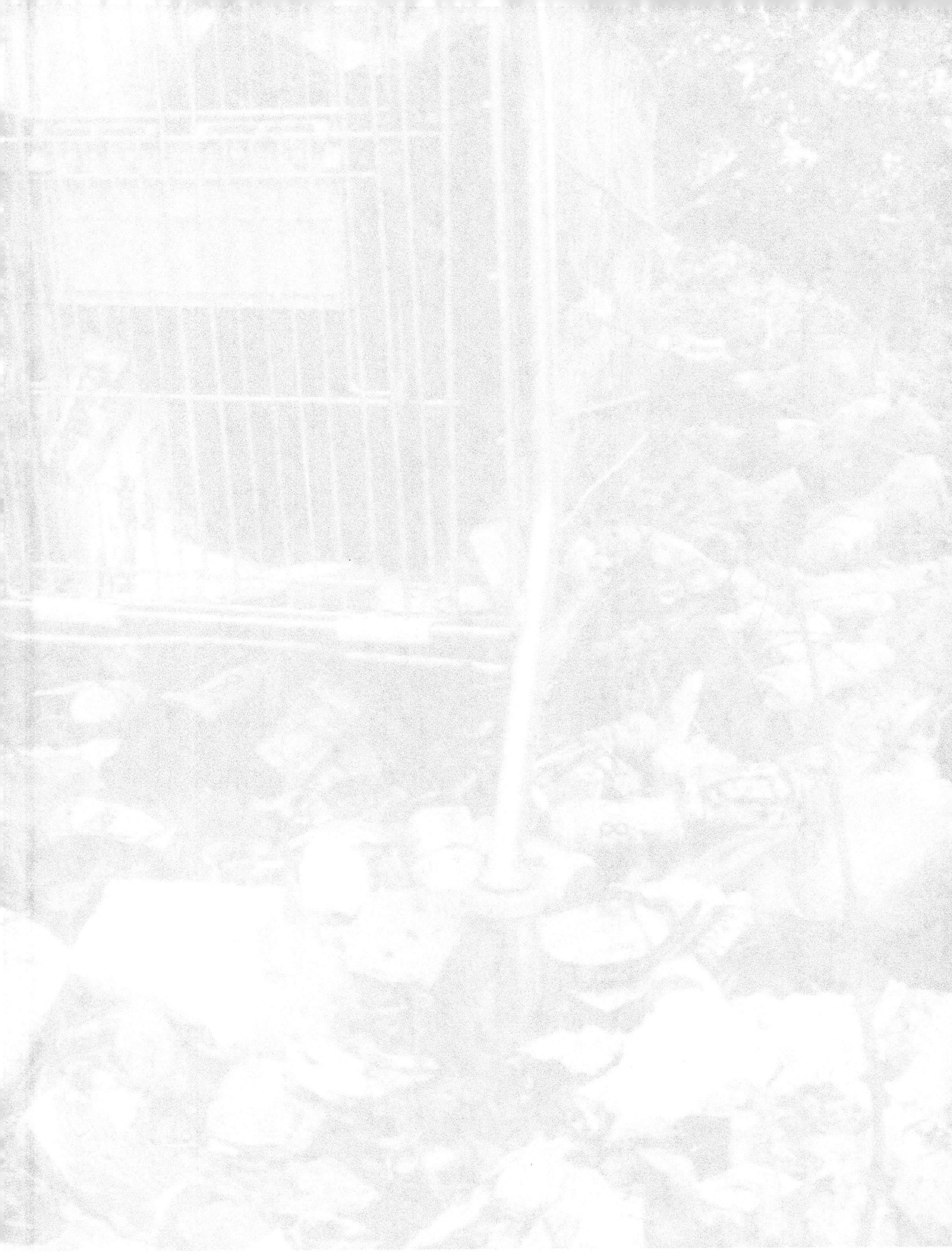

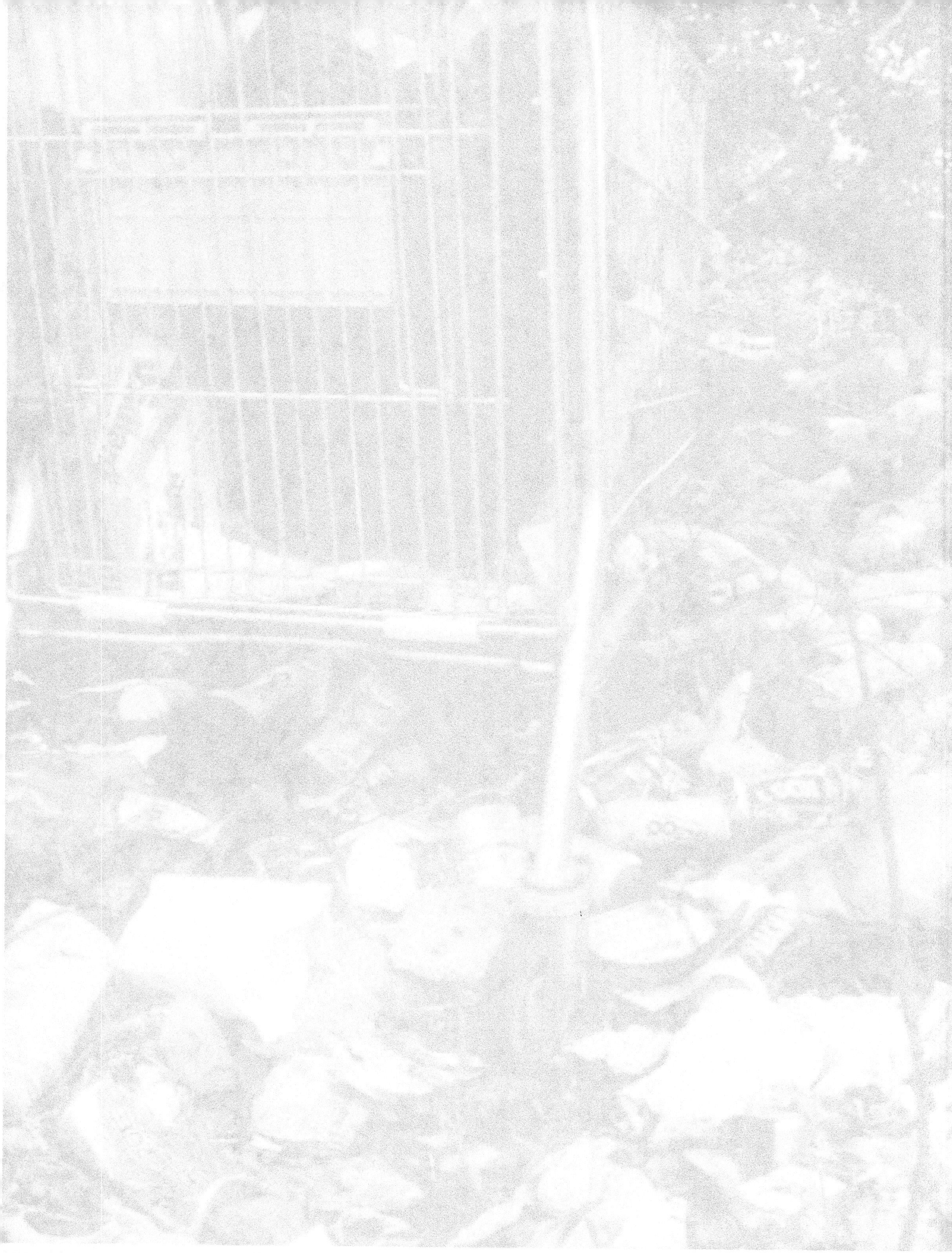

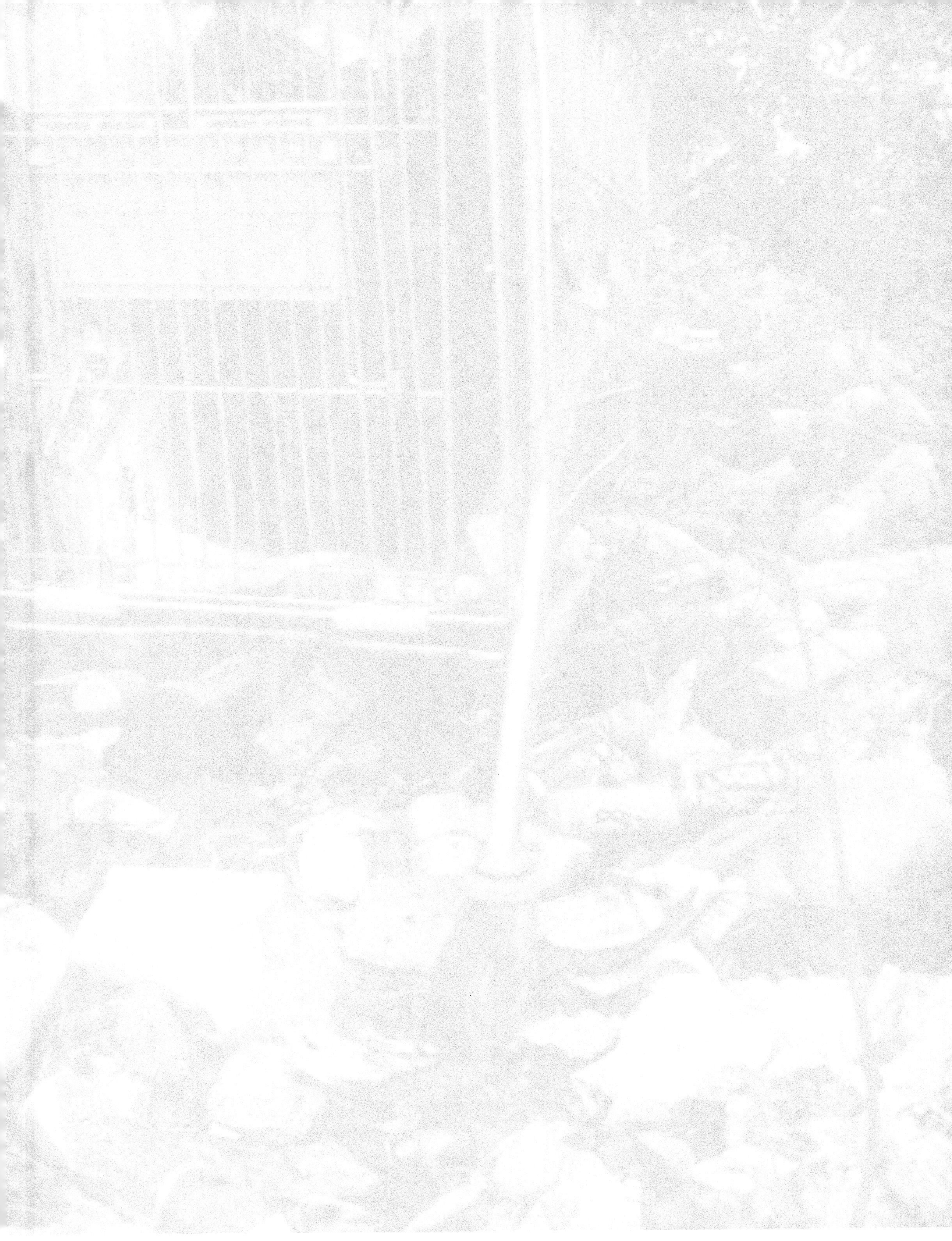

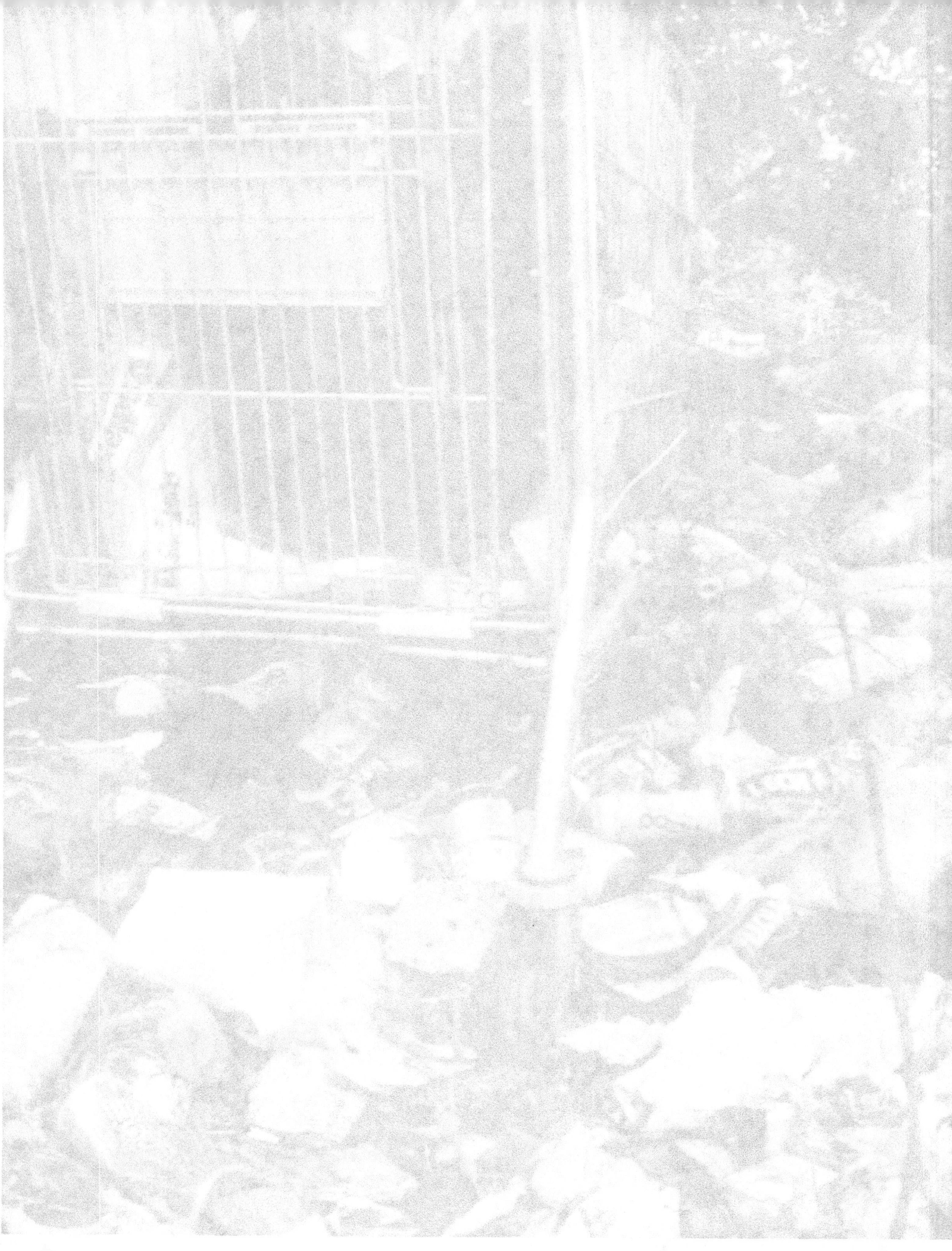

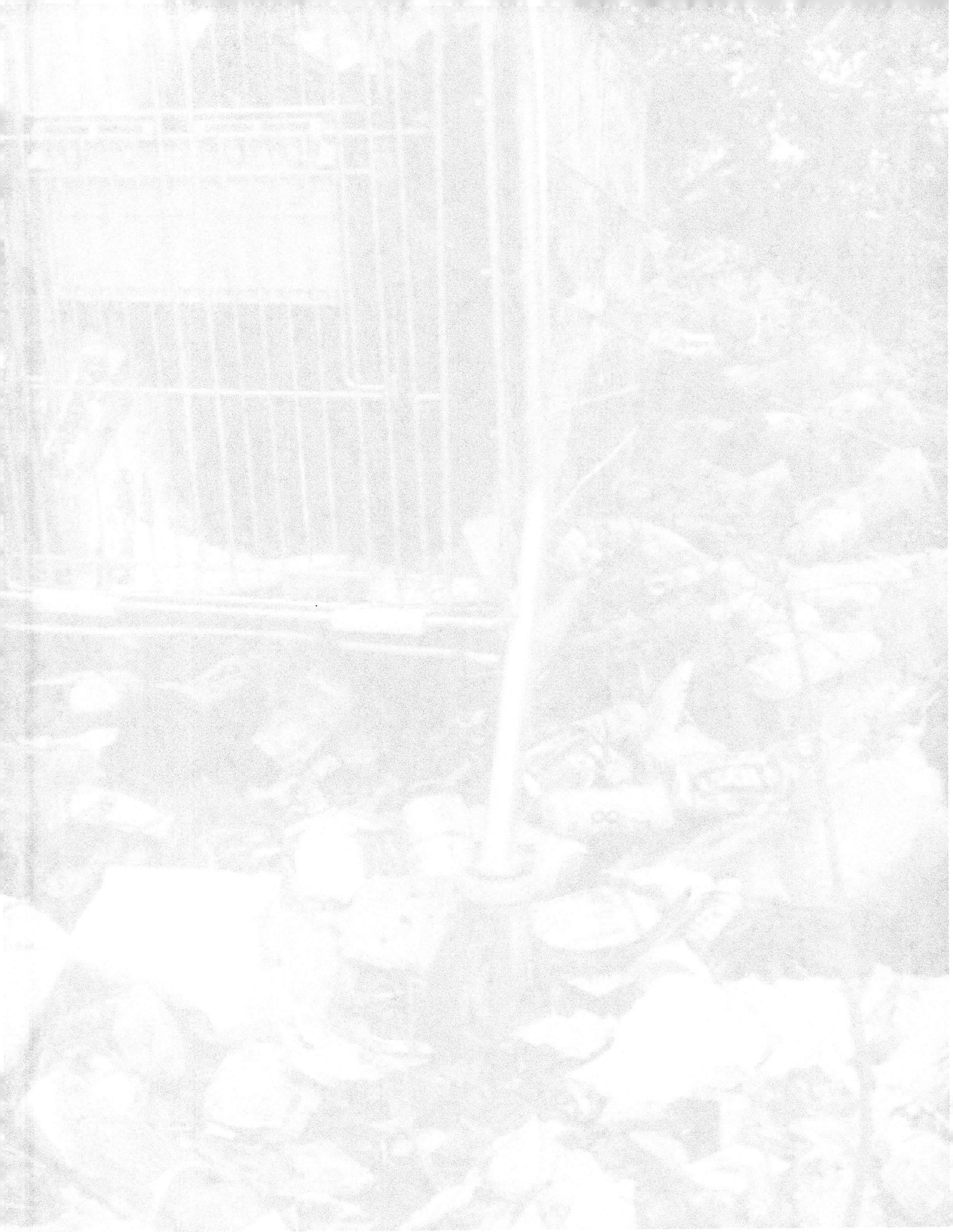

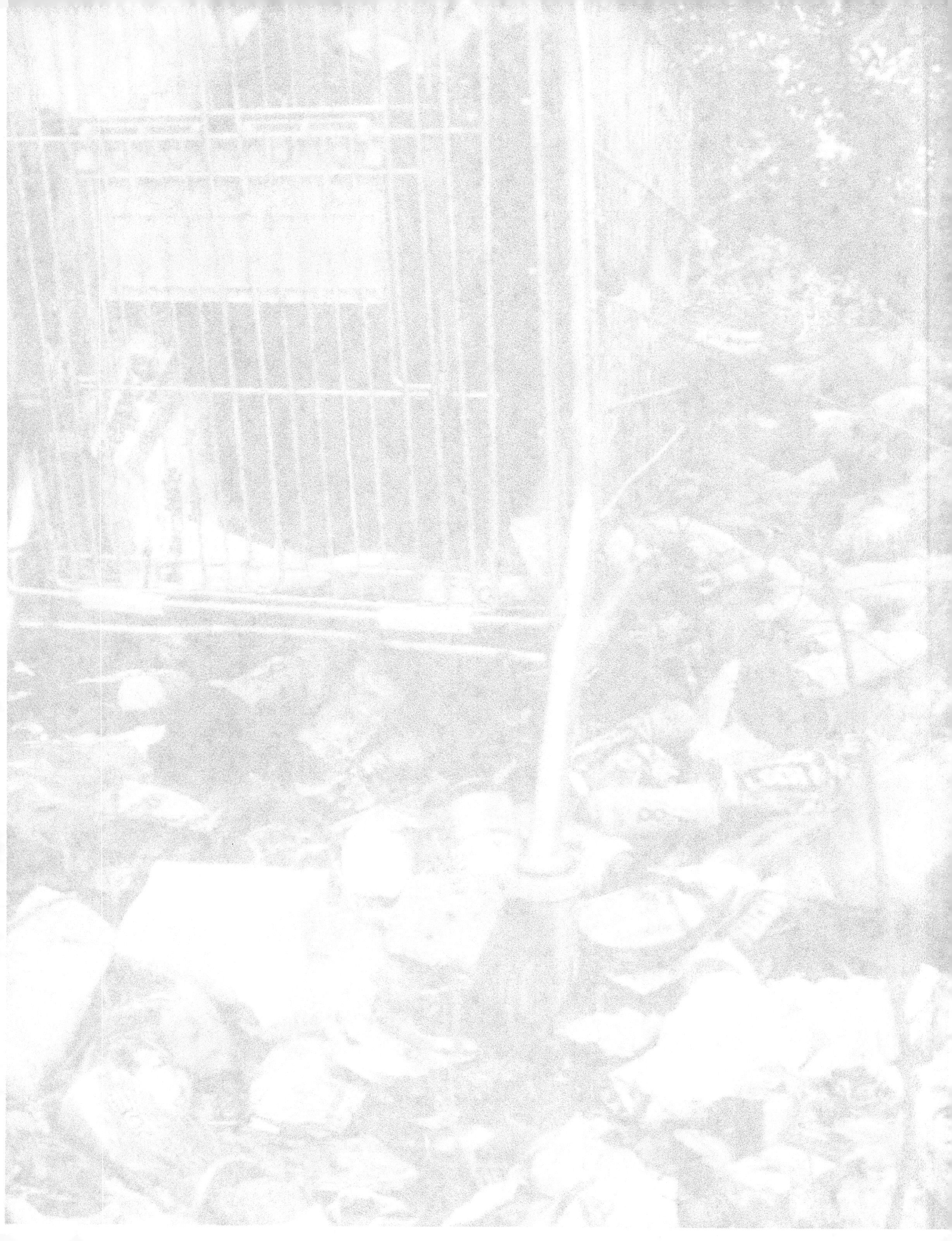

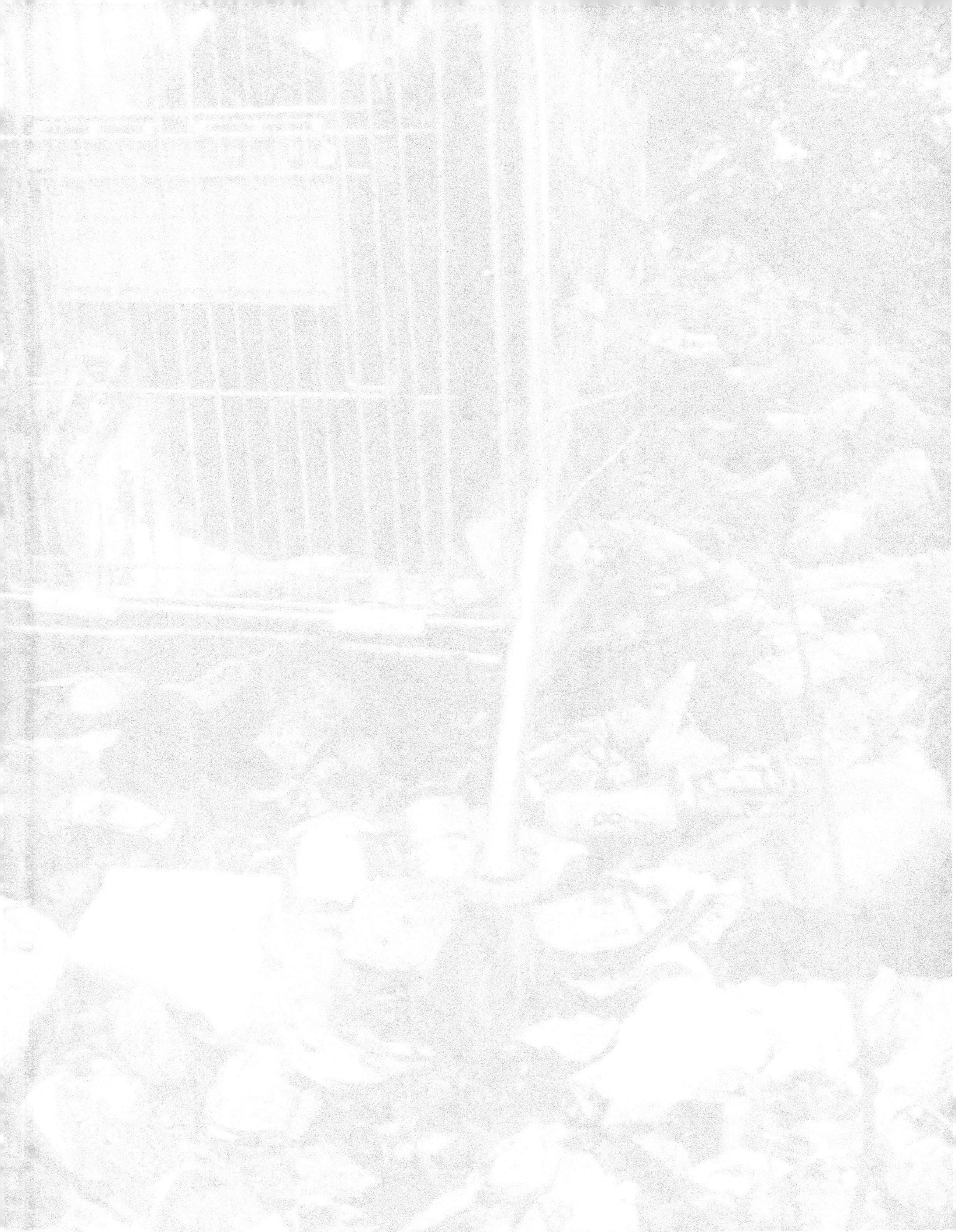

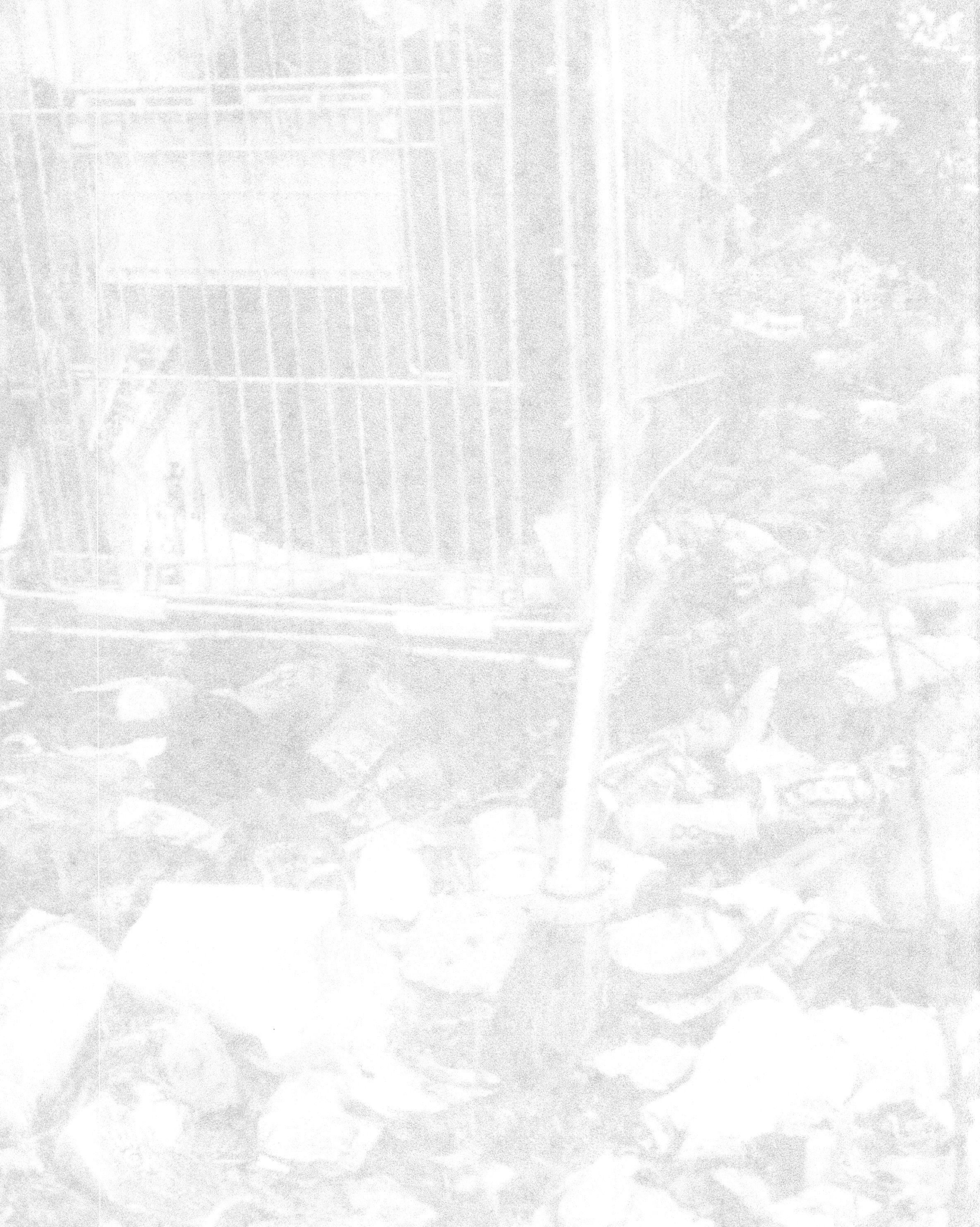

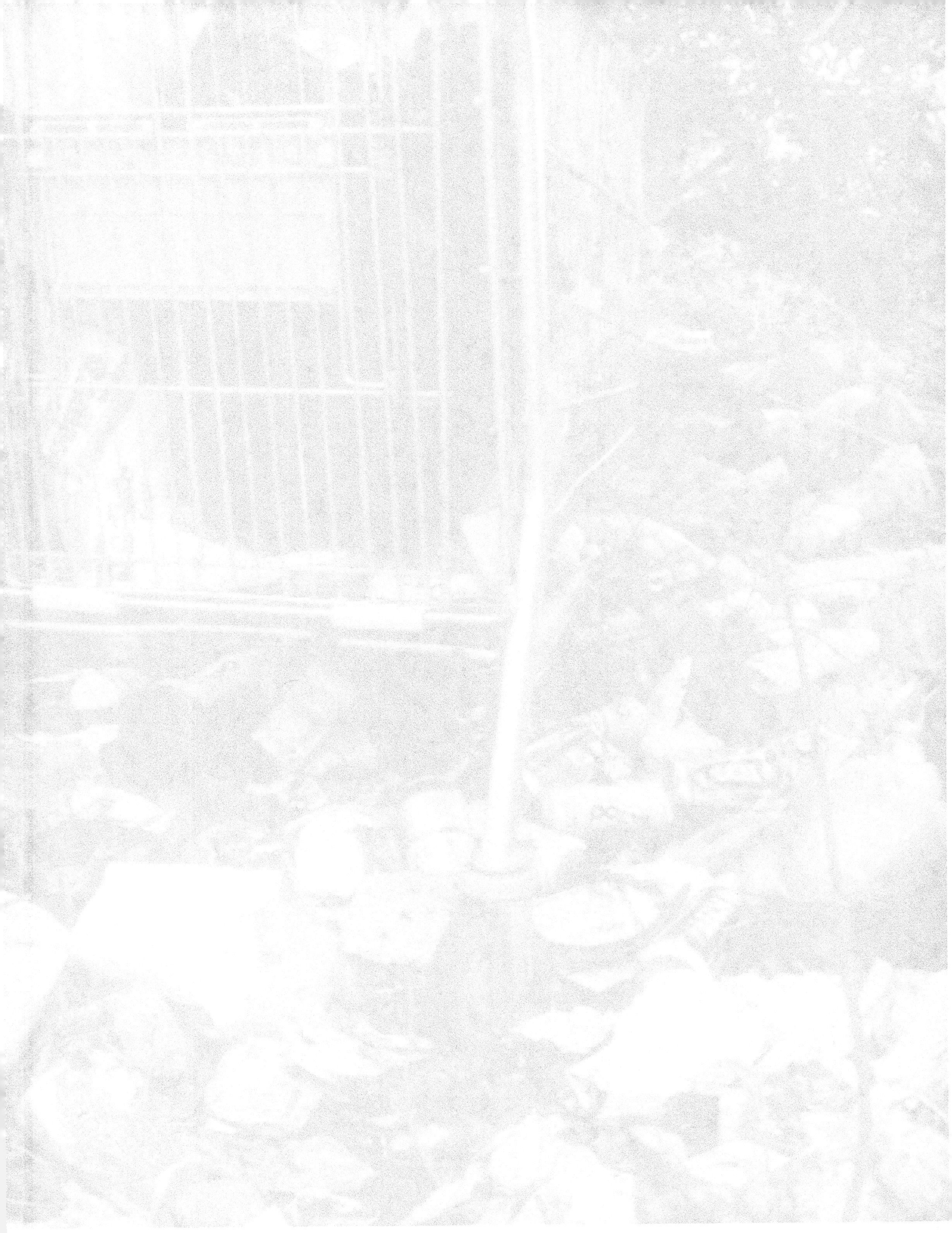

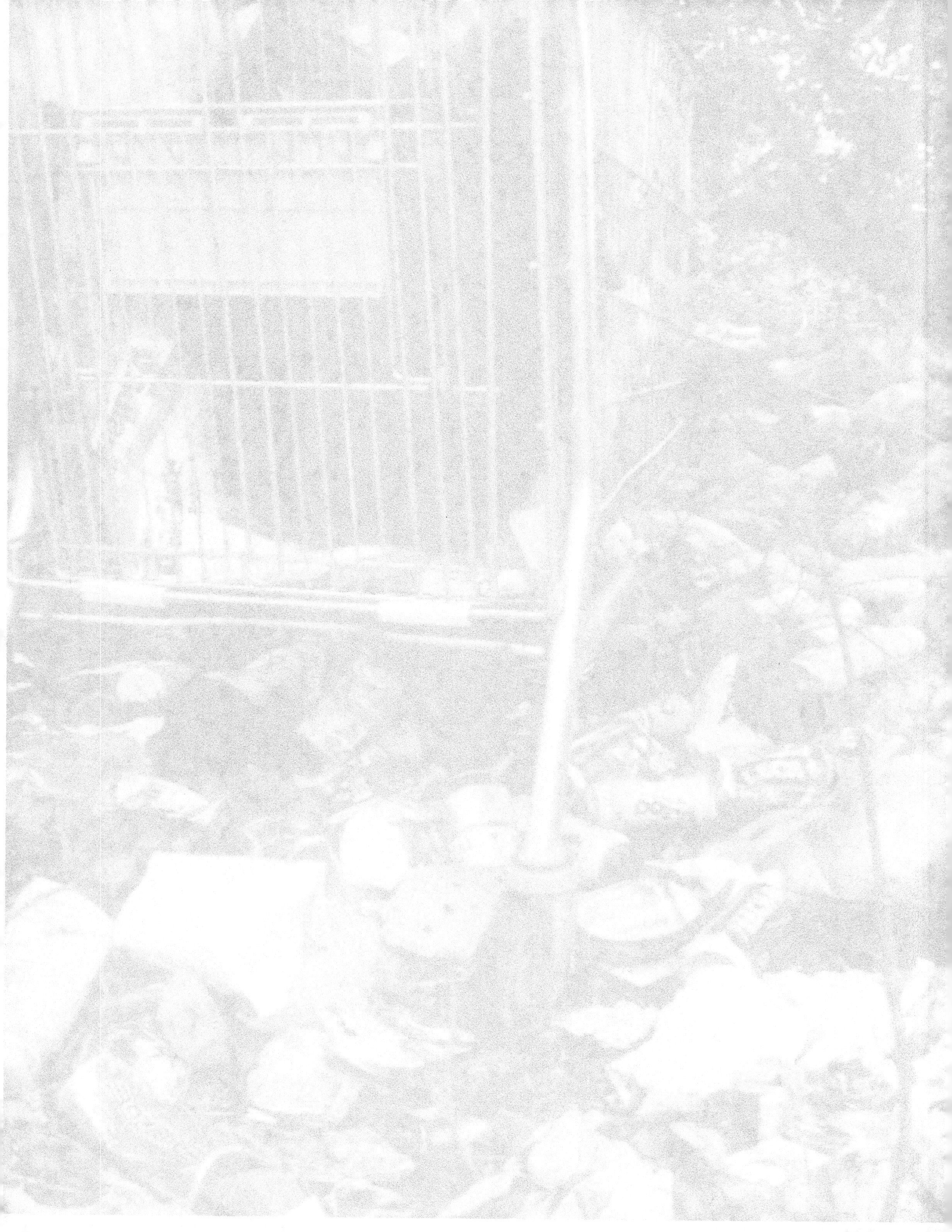

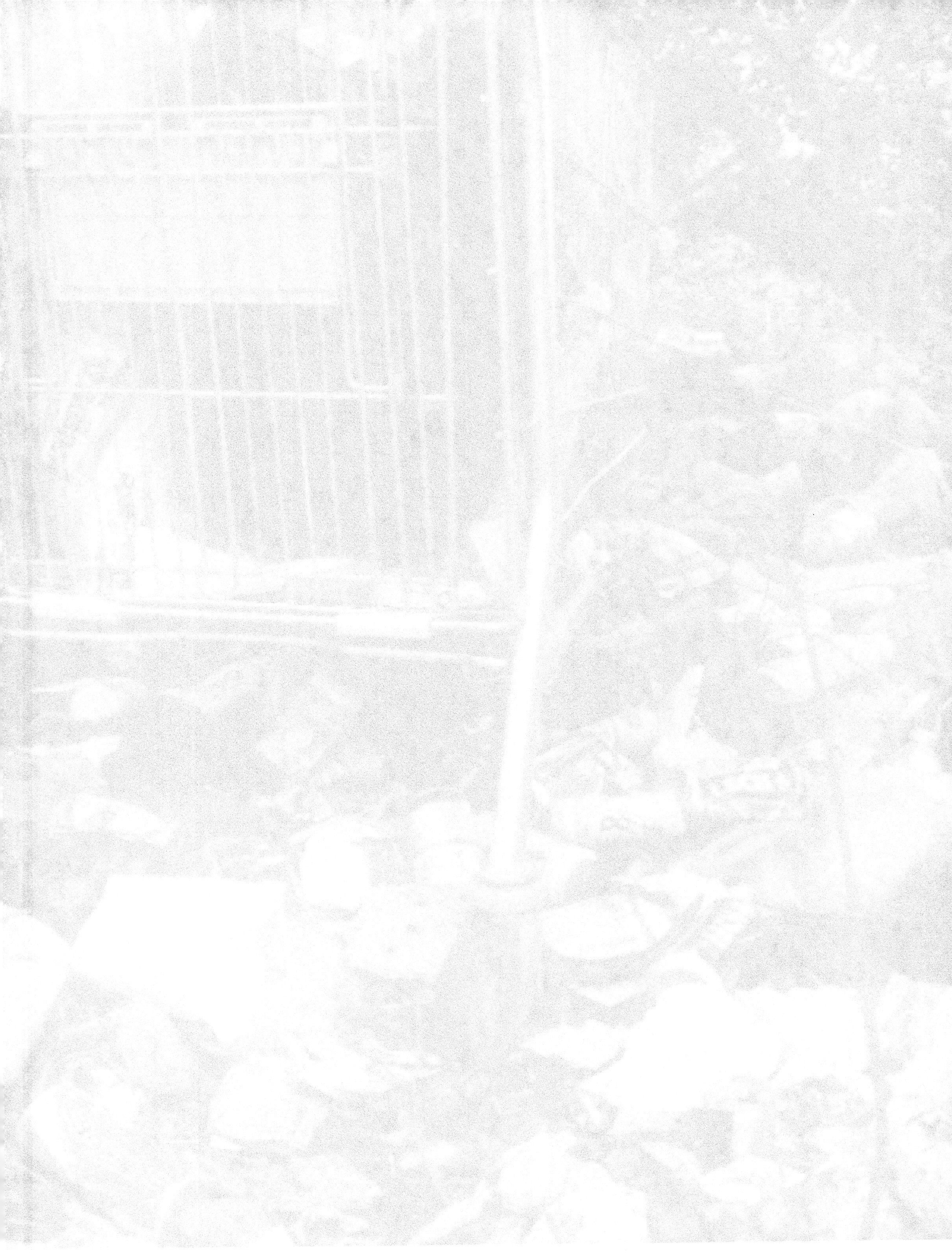

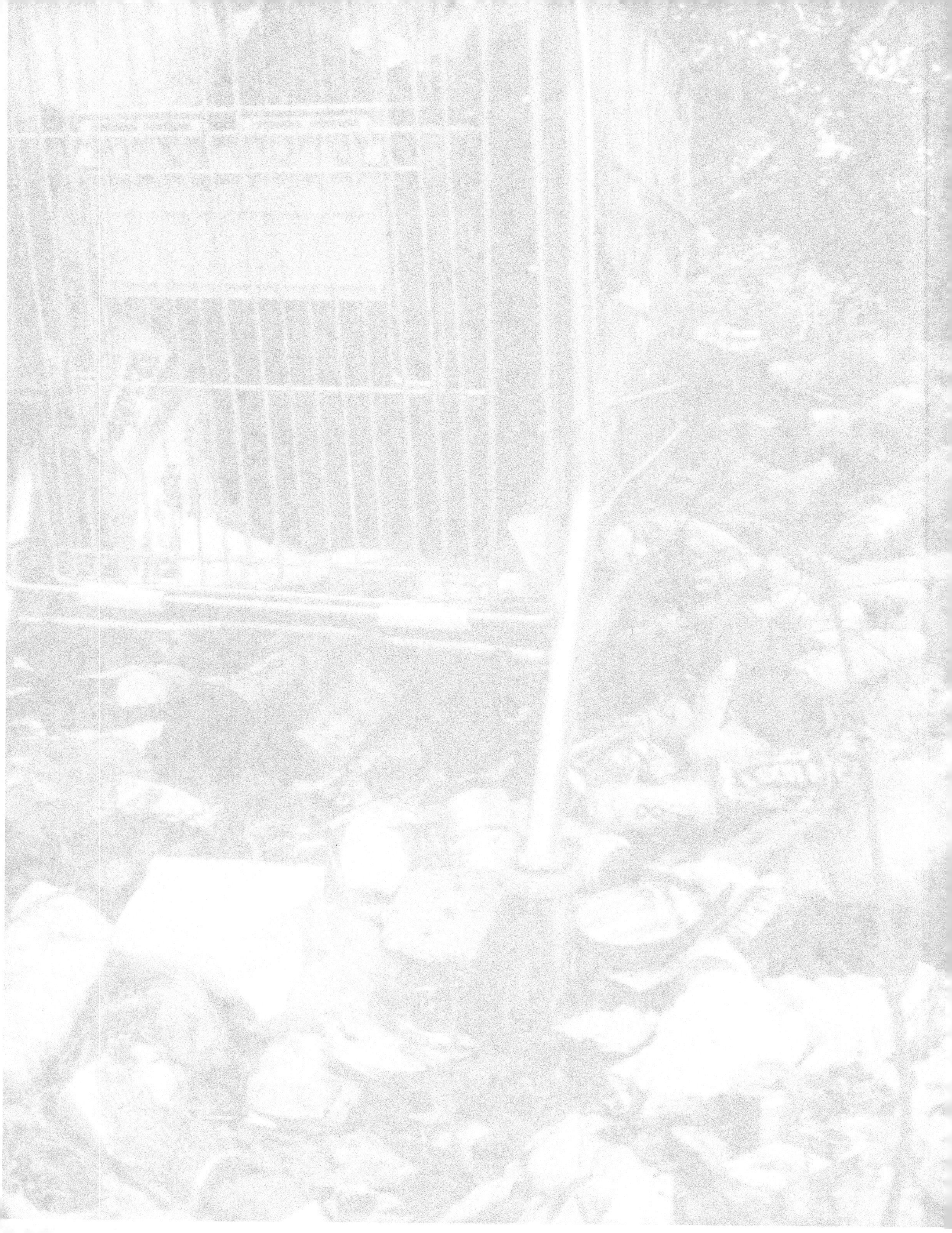

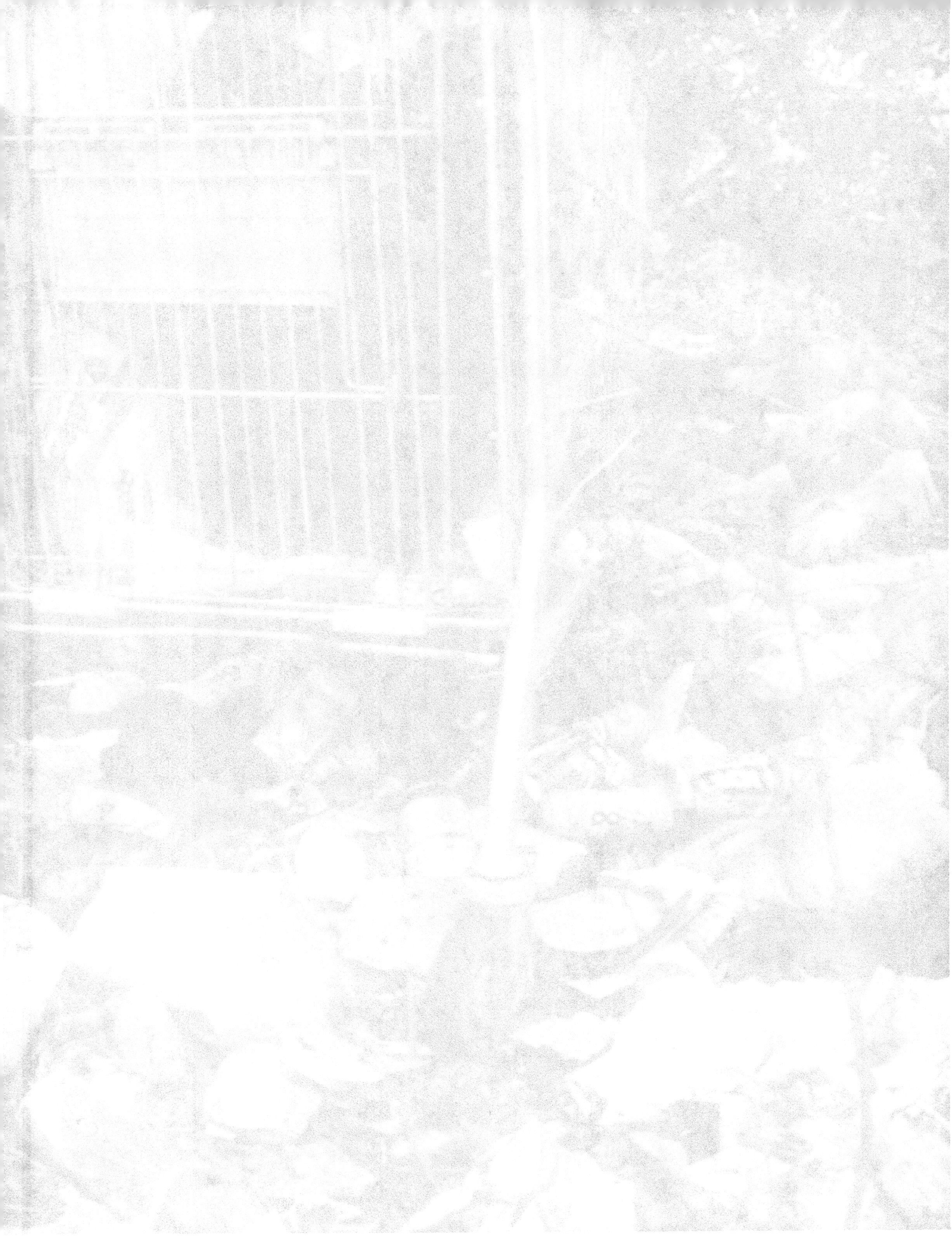

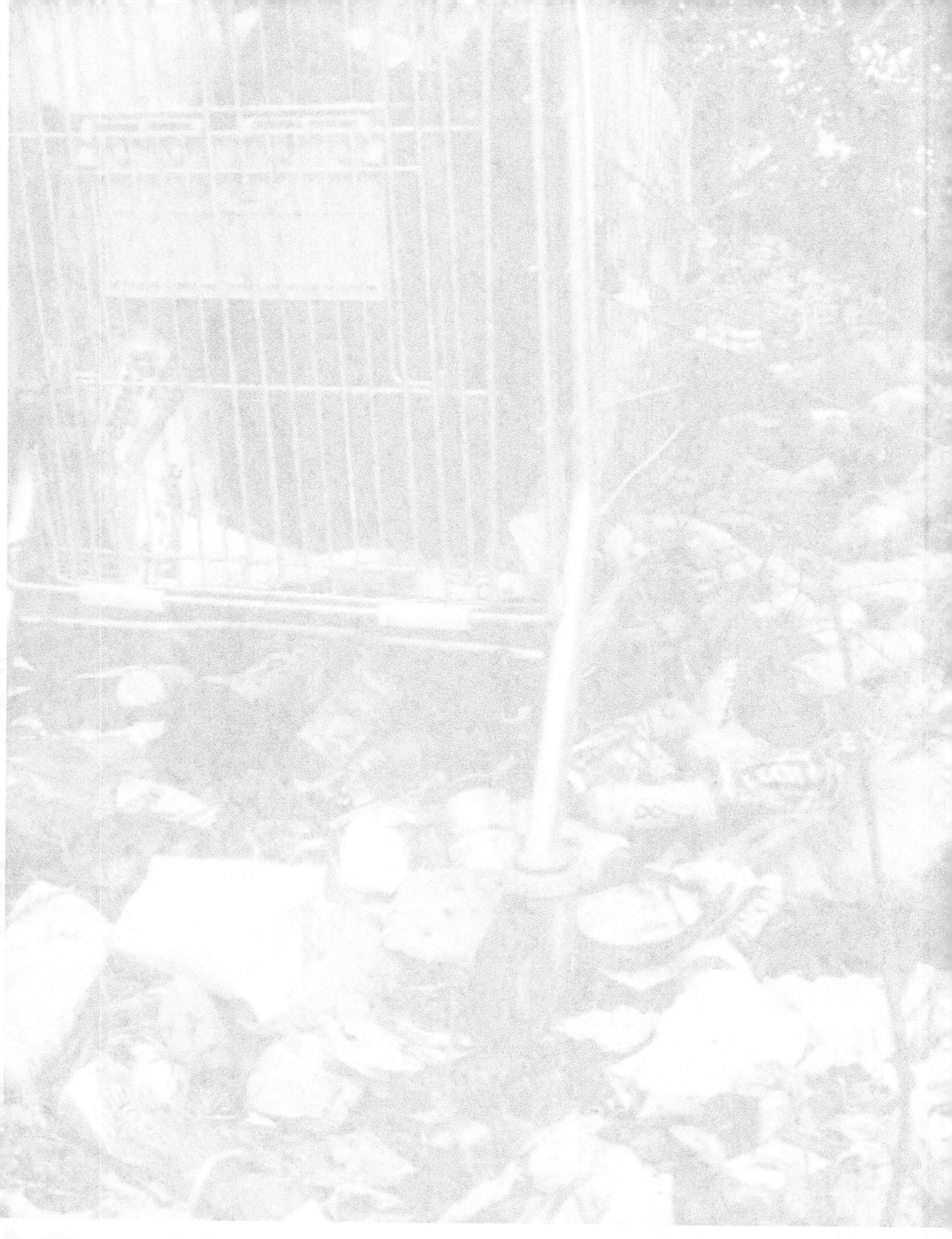

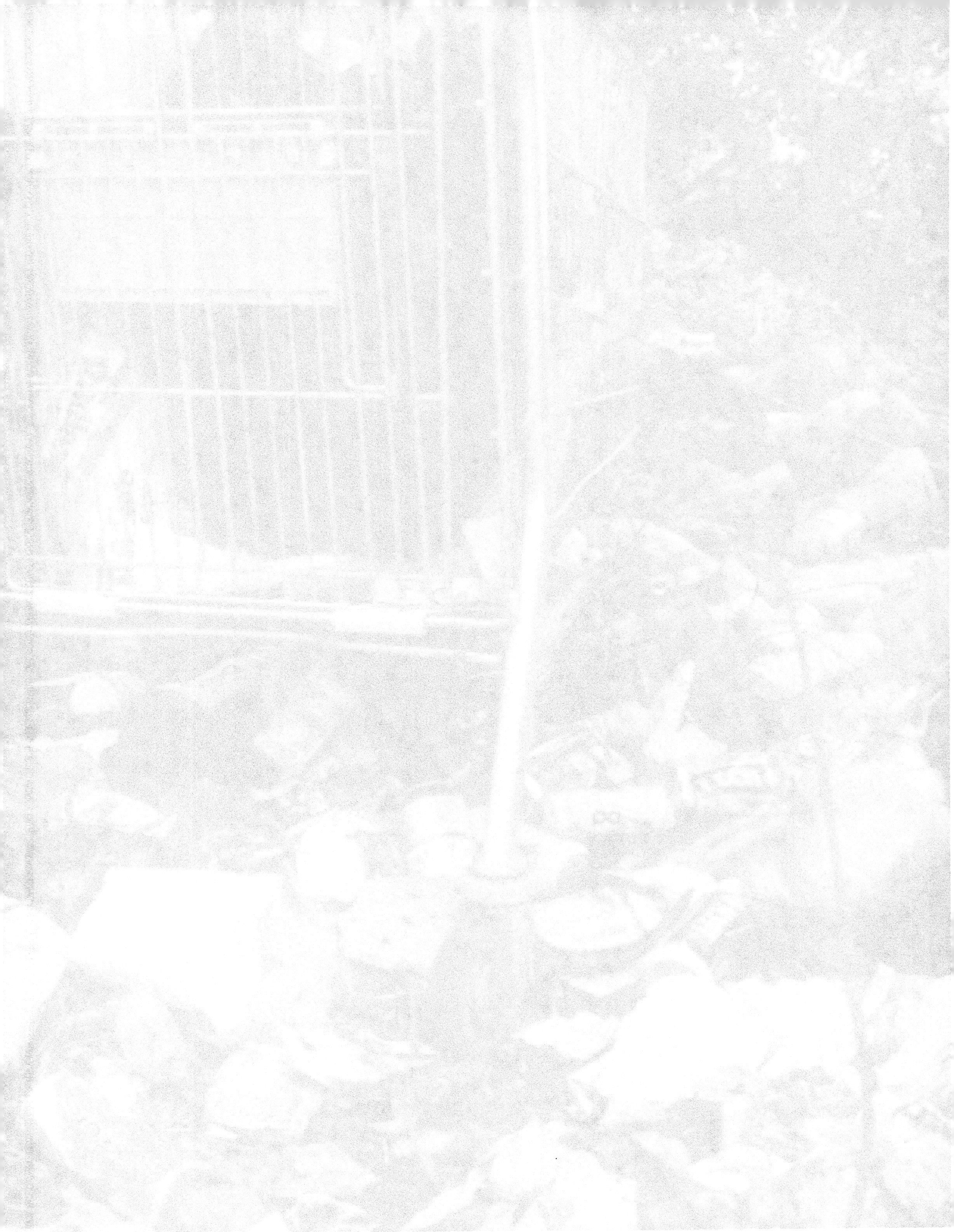

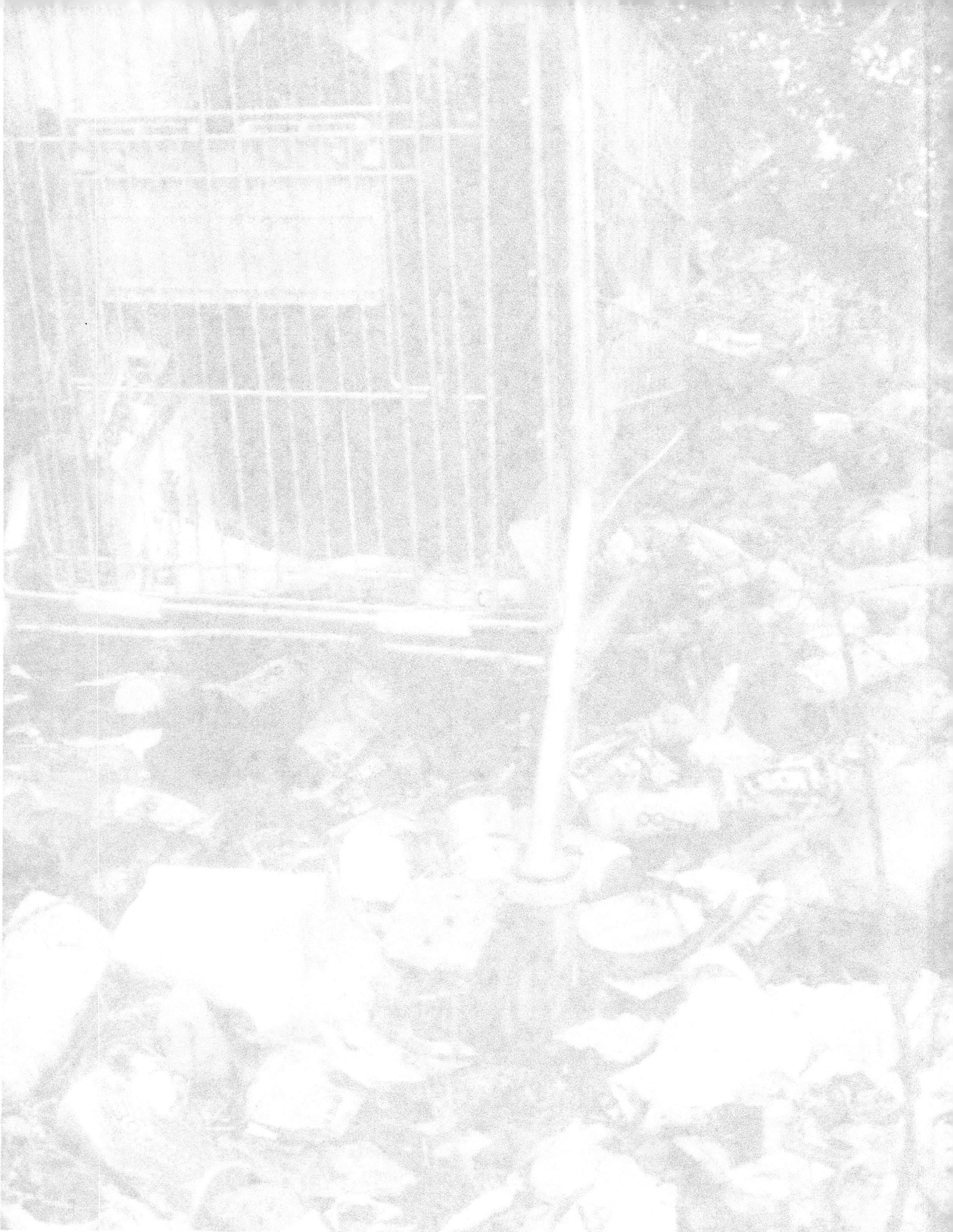

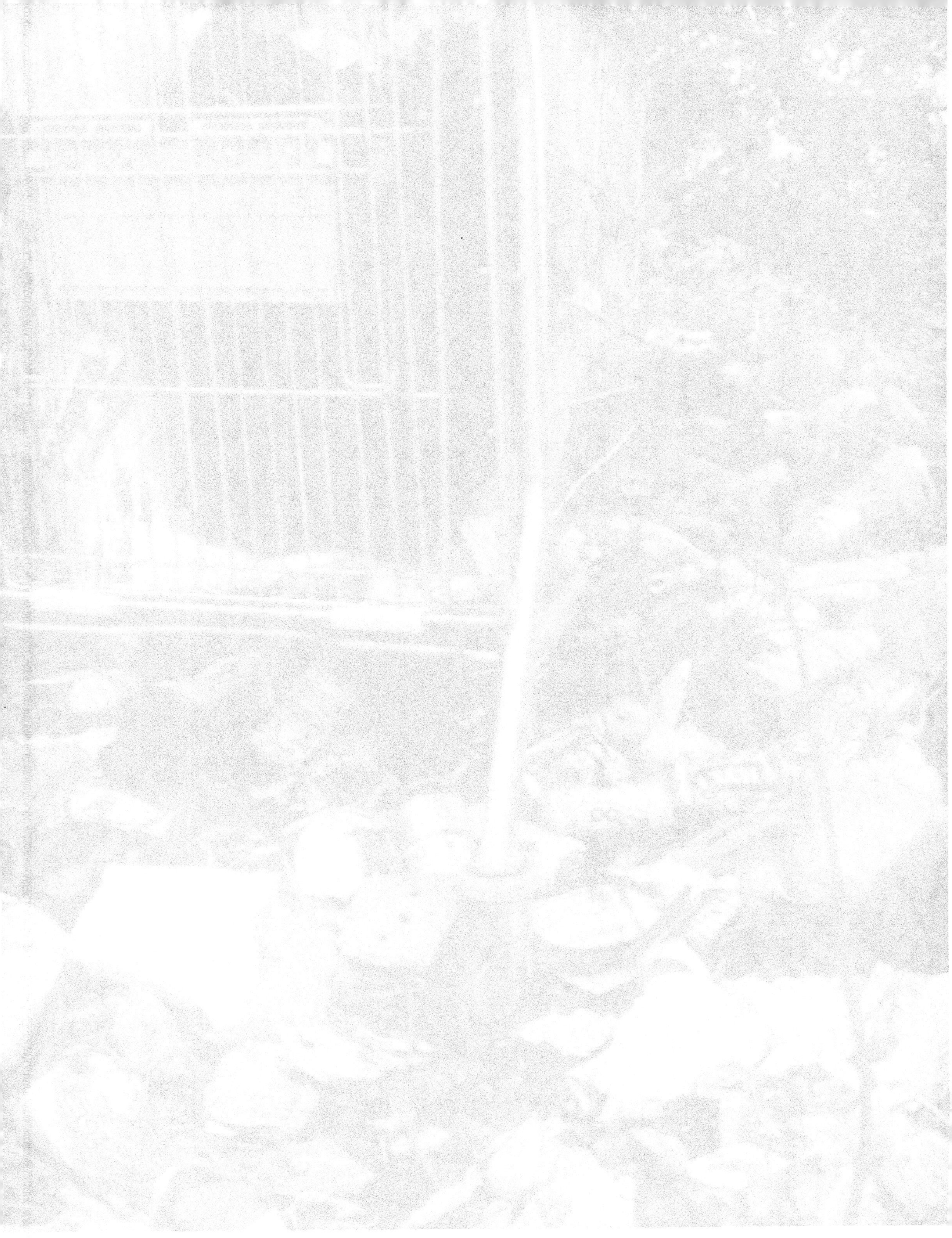

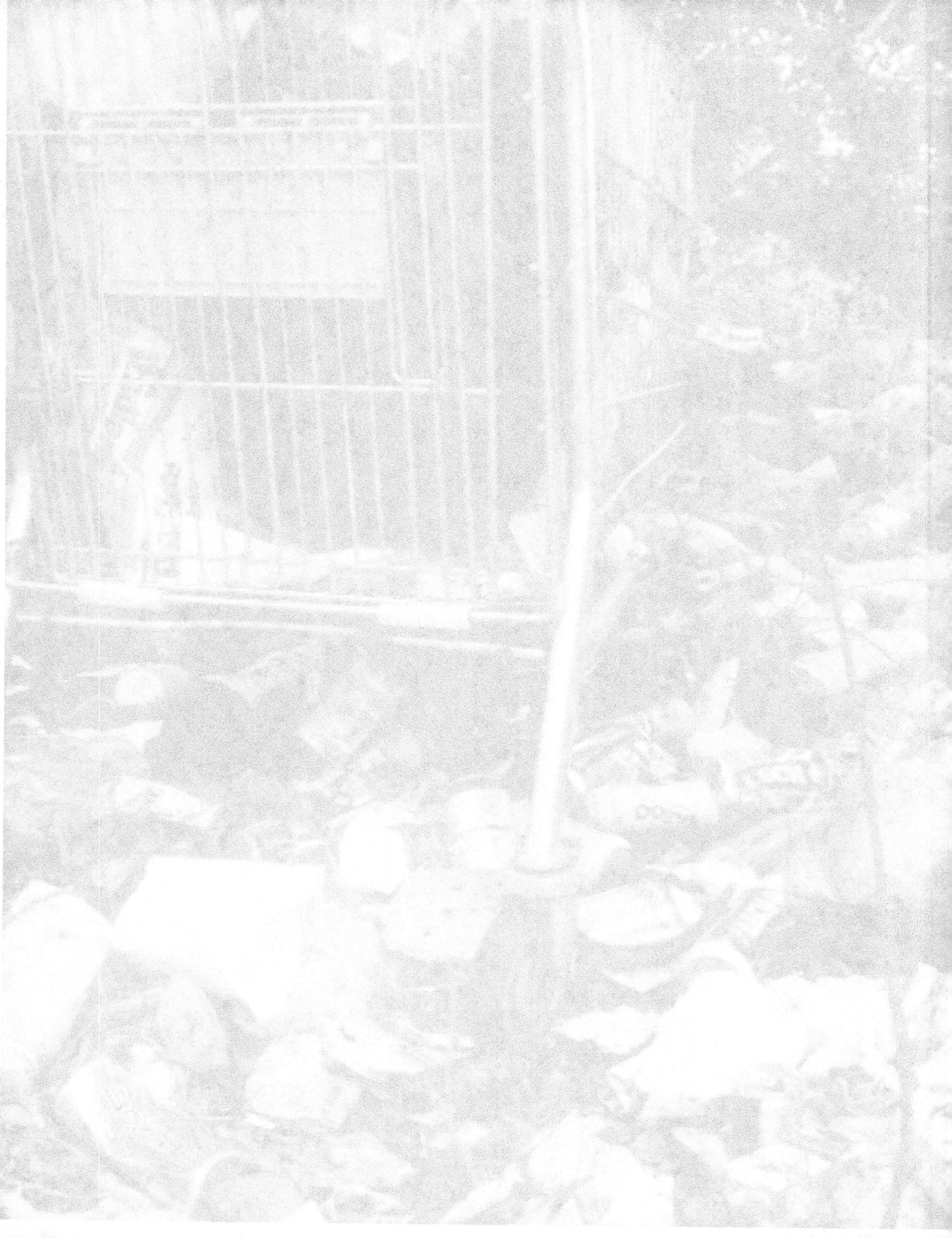

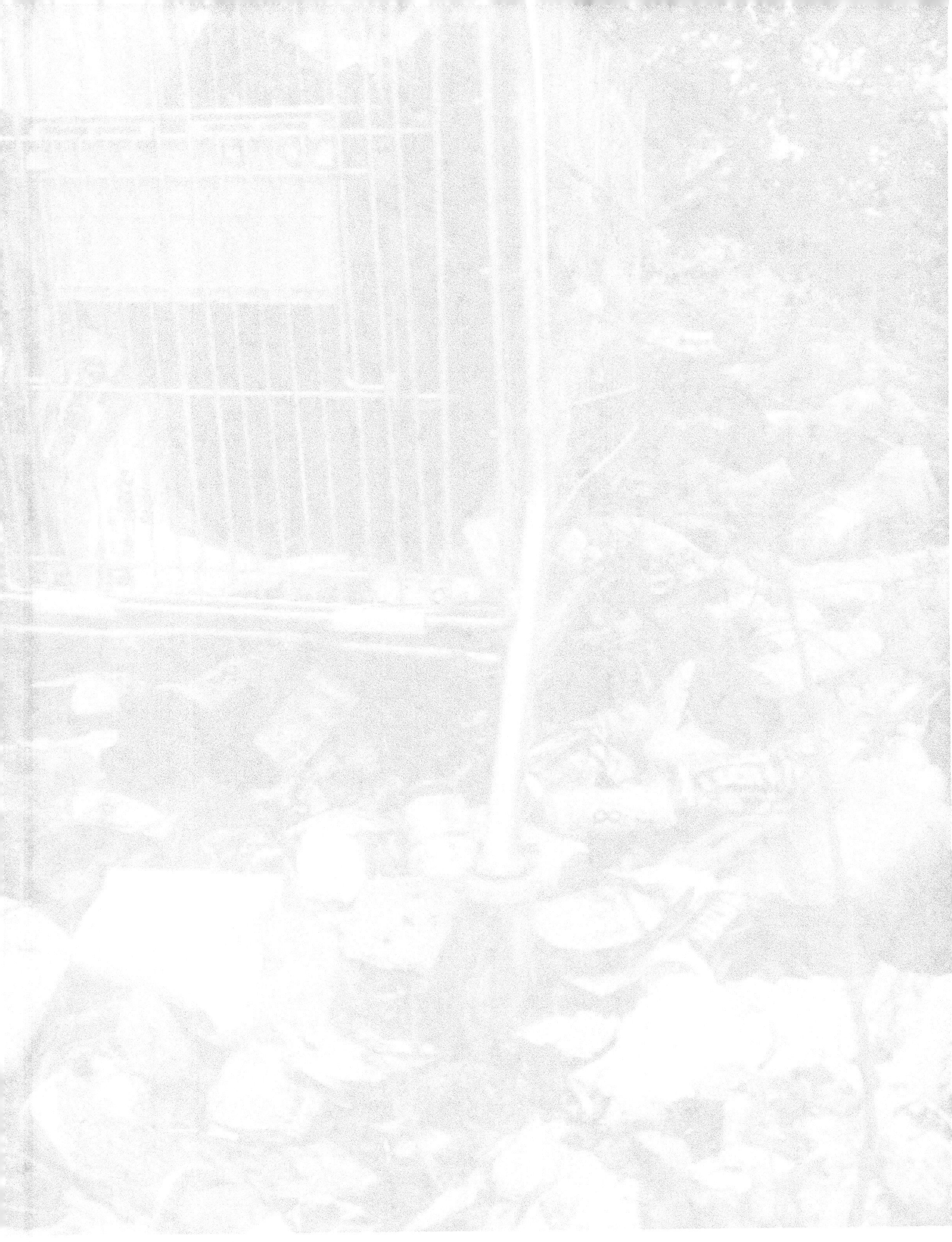

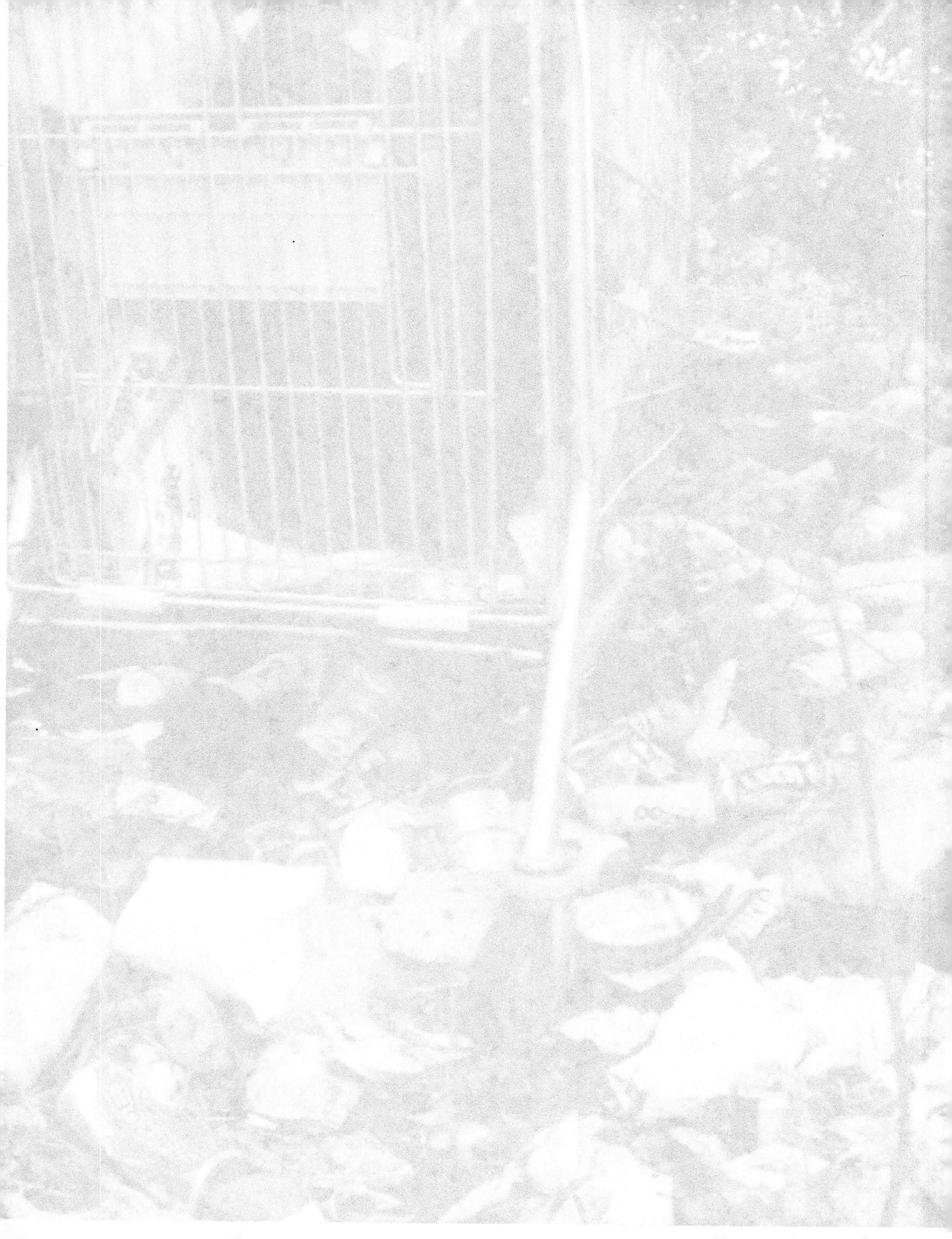

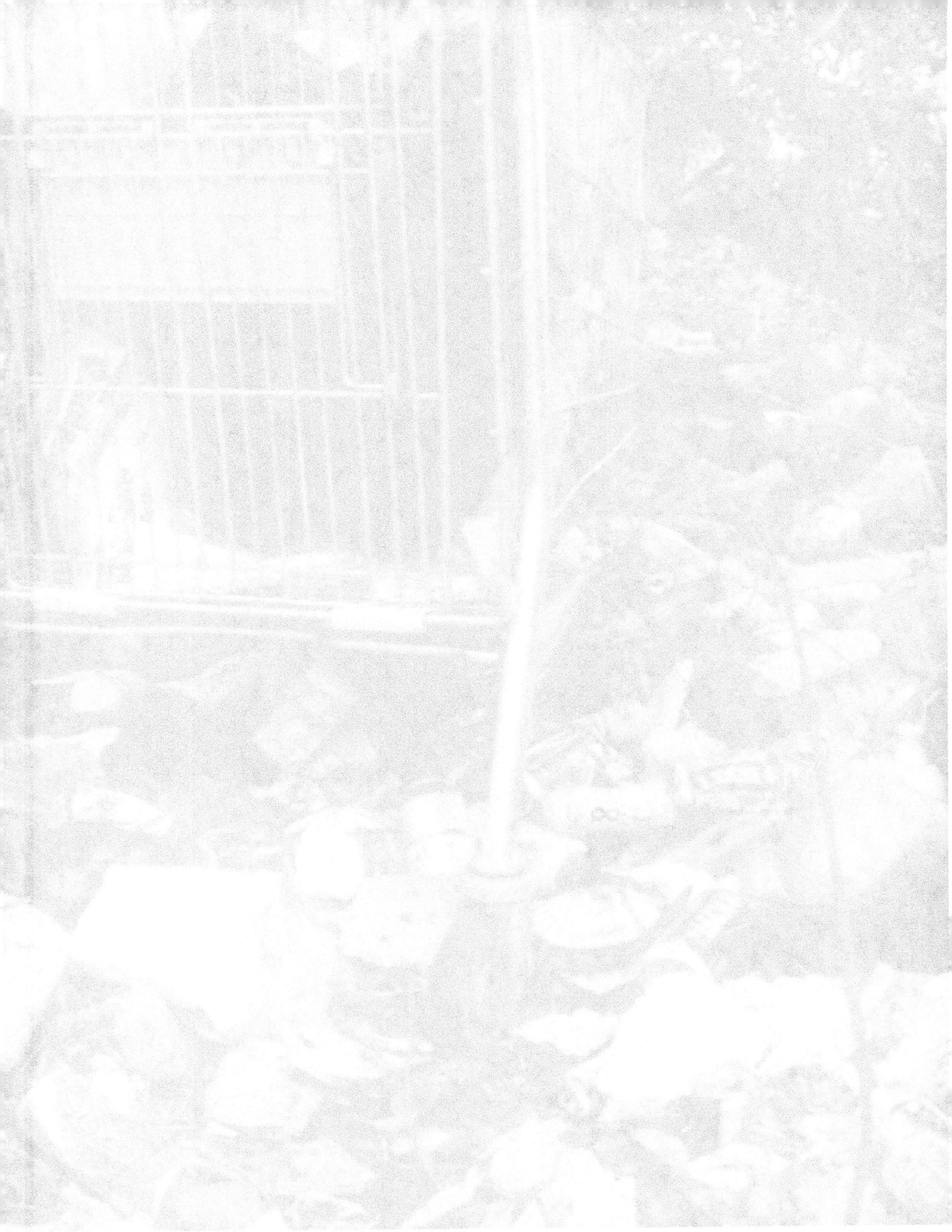

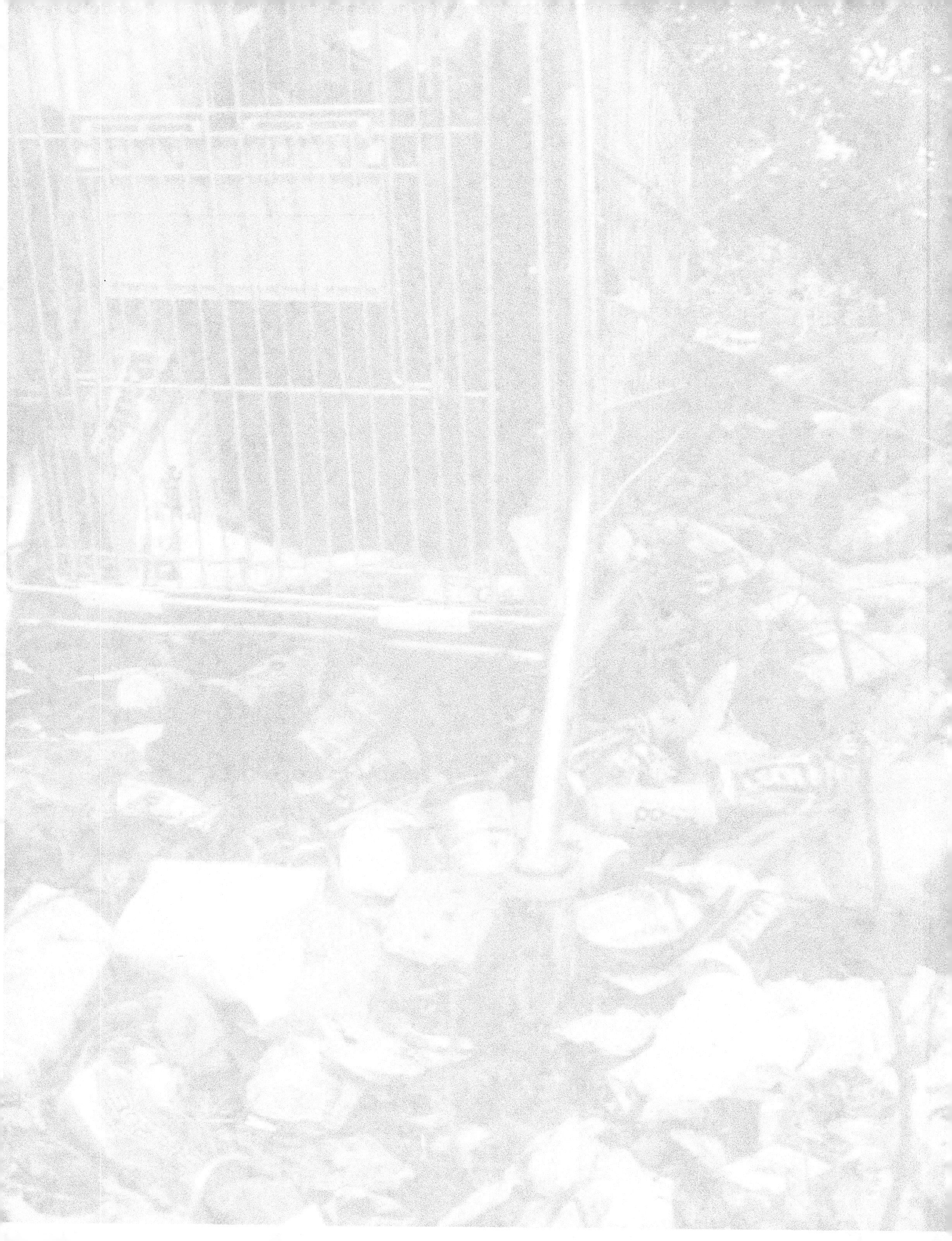

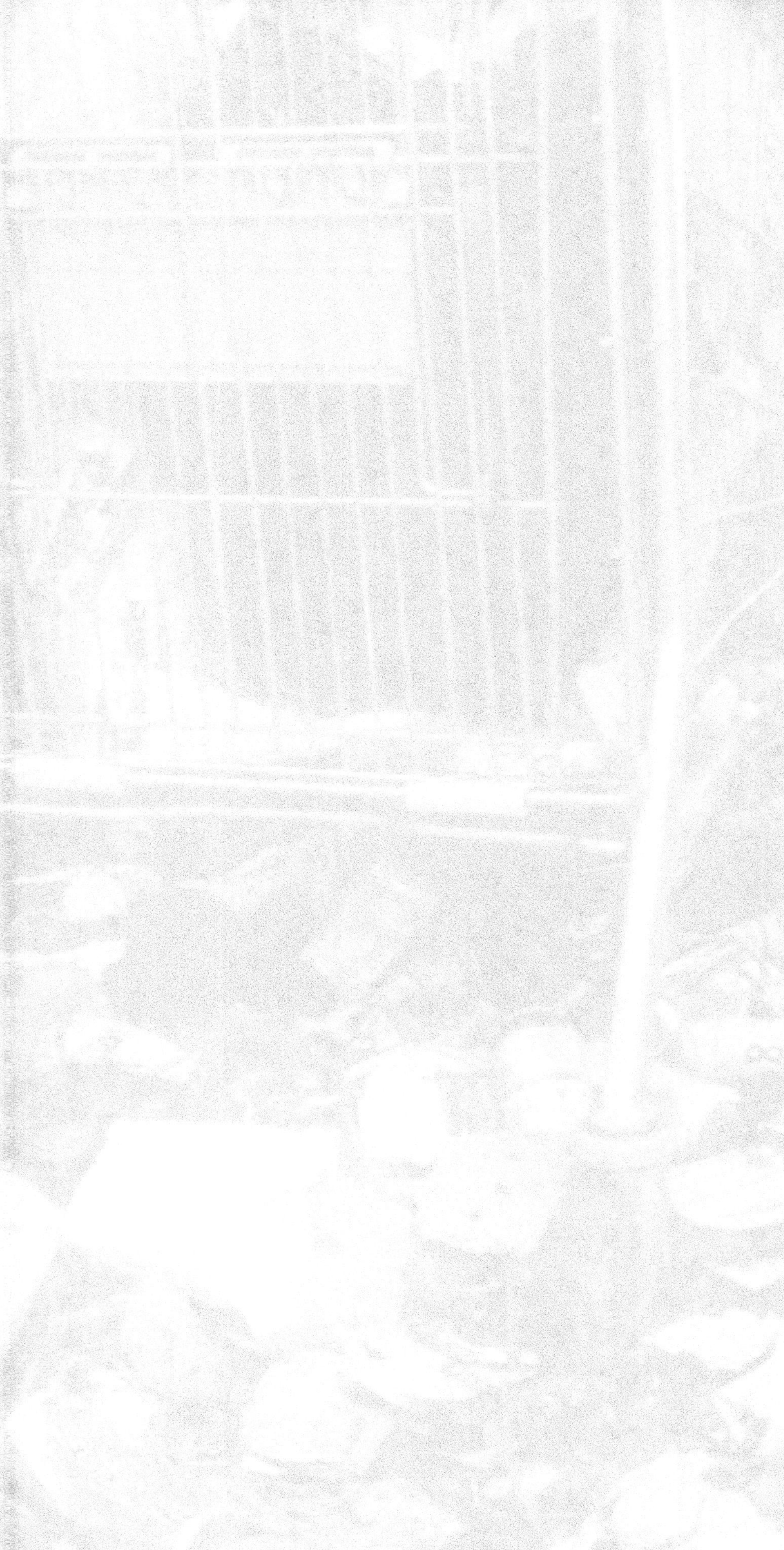

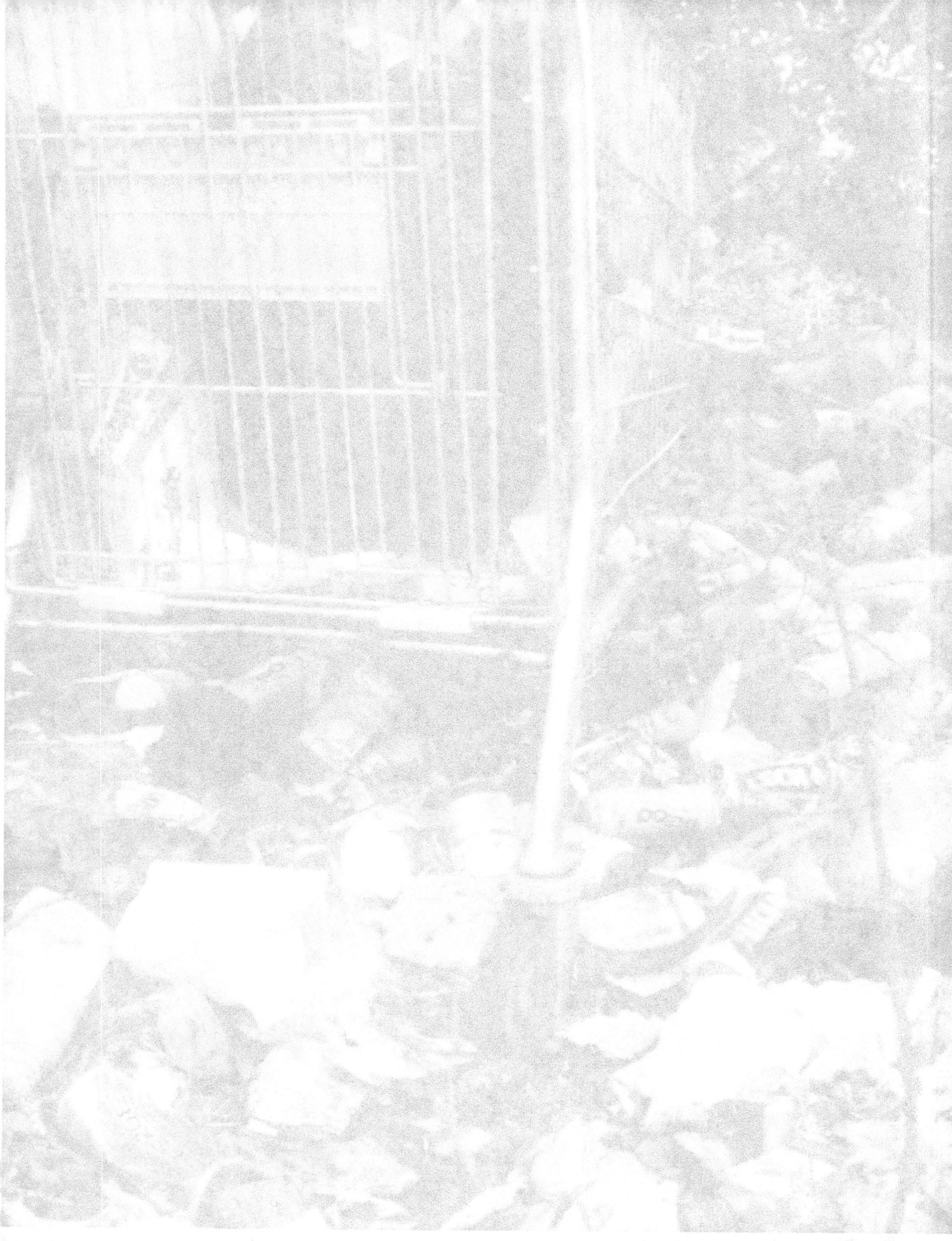

www.ingramcontent.com/pod-product-compliance
Lightning Source LLC
Chambersburg PA
CBHW080400030726
47598CB00010B/2826

* 9 7 8 1 6 3 6 5 7 2 8 8 8 *